F
1

Reading and Writing for Today's Adults

Voyager

Advisers to the Series

Mary Dunn Siedow
Director
North Carolina Literacy Resource Center
Raleigh, NC

Linda Thistlethwaite
Associate Director
The Central Illinois Adult Education Service Center
Western Illinois University
Macomb, IL

Reviewer

Linda J. Church
Director, Research and Development
Laubach Literacy Action
Syracuse, NY

New Readers Press

Contributing Writers

Foundation Book **Teacher's Notes:** Linda J. Church, Pamela Bliss

Voyager 1 **Teacher's Notes:** Christy M. Newman

ISBN 978-1-56420-159-1

Copyright © 2000 New Readers Press
New Readers Press
A Publishing Division of ProLiteracy
1320 Jamesville Avenue, Syracuse, New York 13210
www.newreaderspress.com

Printed in the United States of America
9   8   7   6   5

All proceeds from the sale of New Readers Press materials
support literacy programs in the United States and worldwide.

Director of Acquisitions and Development: Christina Jagger
Content Editor: Mary Hutchison
Developer: Learning Unlimited, Oak Park, IL
Developmental Editor: Sarah Conroy Williams
Cover Designer: Gerald Russell
Designer: Kimbrly Koennecke

ProLiteracy Worldwide and New Readers Press are not owned or sponsored by Voyager Expanded Learning, Inc.

Contents

Overview of the Series

Voyager: Reading and Writing for Today's Adults is a four-stage program that utilizes contemporary content and instructional approaches to teach the reading, writing, critical thinking, and communication skills that adults need in today's world. It takes students from the beginning stages of reading and writing through the ninth-grade level.

The *Voyager* series consists of nine student books, nine workbooks, four teacher's resource guides, and a placement tool.

▶ Key Features and Benefits

1. ***Voyager* integrates contemporary content and instructional approaches with the best elements from traditional instruction and practice.** In the early books, phonics and other word recognition strategies are combined with reading comprehension instruction. Later books emphasize comprehension and meaning. Instruction in the writing process is combined with instruction in spelling, capitalization, punctuation, grammar, usage, and sentence structure. This balanced approach results in a solid, effective program.

2. **Each lesson integrates reading, writing, listening, speaking, and thinking skills.** Research has shown that literacy development is enhanced when students have the opportunity to apply all these skills to a single topic. Activities and skill-building exercises in *Voyager* are related to the topic of the reading selection, the core of the lesson.

3. ***Voyager* is theme-based.** In *Foundation Book,* each lesson has a theme. The other eight student books are divided into four units, each with its own theme. This theme-based approach encourages students to delve into a topic using a variety of approaches. As students complete the reading, writing, and thinking activities in a unit, they have opportunities to examine the common concepts and issues associated with that unit's theme.

4. **Students work with authentic reading selections and writing assignments—practical,** informational, and literary. *Voyager* draws from a combination of high-quality literature, information-rich articles, adult student writings, and the types of forms, documents, and graphic material adults commonly encounter. Working with these materials, students achieve success at both academic and everyday reading and writing activities.

5. **Activities in *Voyager* give students opportunities to work both independently and collaboratively.** Students complete some activities by themselves. In other activities, students participate in discussions, group problem solving, and so on. These varied ways of working reflect daily life.

6. ***Voyager* can be successfully used in a variety of settings.** *Voyager* can be used in large- or small-group instructional programs, in one-on-one tutorial situations, and independently for self-study in an individualized or learning lab program. This flexible instructional format meets the needs of a wide variety of programs.

7. ***Voyager* provides additional support for both students and teachers.** Workbooks, one for each student book, are filled with exercises that give students extra practice with the major skills taught in the lessons. Teacher's resource guides provide valuable additional background information, teaching ideas, and photocopy masters (PCMs). These support materials save time by helping teachers create lesson plans and reinforcement materials.

▶ A Closer Look at *Voyager* Components

▶ **Nine student books** form the instructional core of the *Voyager* program.

▶ **Nine workbooks,** one for each student book, provide students with extra skills practice.

▶ **Four teacher's resource guides,** one for each stage, contain a general overview and orientation to each stage, lesson-by-lesson teacher's notes and extension activities for the student books, and PCMs for both instruction and assessment.

▶ **The placement tool** helps teachers place students in the appropriate *Voyager* student book.

The Four Stages

The *Voyager* series is a four-stage program. Each stage of *Voyager* reflects a separate stage of reading and writing development. Thus, each stage has its own emphasis and design. The four stages are

1. **Learning to Read** (Reading levels 0.5–2.5) Emphasis at this stage is on short reading selections containing common words; phonics instruction; and writing, speaking, and listening activities to teach basic skills and build confidence.

2. **The Emerging Reader** (Reading levels 2.0–4.5) Emphasis at this stage is on literary and informational reading selections; phonics and other word recognition strategies; comprehension and critical thinking strategies; and writing, speaking, and listening skills.

3. **Reading to Learn** (Reading levels 4.0–7.5) Emphasis at this stage is on expanding students' reading, thinking, writing, and oral communication skills, using reading materials typically found at home, at work, at school, and in the community.

4. **Reading for Work and Life** (Reading levels 7.0–9.5) Emphasis at this stage is on having students learn and apply reading, thinking, writing, and oral communications skills through themes and readings that are work- and life-oriented.

Components of the Voyager Series

Stages	Student Books (96 – 176 pages)	Reading Levels	Workbooks (48 pages each)	Teacher's Resource Guides
Learning to Read	Voyager Foundation Book (96 pages)	0.5 – 1.5	Voyager Foundation Workbook	Teacher's Resource Guide for Foundation Book and Voyager 1 (80 pages)
	Voyager 1 (128 pages)	1.0 – 2.5	Voyager 1 Workbook	
The Emerging Reader	Voyager 2 (128 pages)	2.0 – 3.5	Voyager 2 Workbook	Teacher's Resource Guide for Voyager 2 and 3 (80 pages)
	Voyager 3 (128 pages)	3.0 – 4.5	Voyager 3 Workbook	
Reading to Learn	Voyager 4 (160 pages)	4.0 – 5.5	Voyager 4 Workbook	Teacher's Resource Guide for Voyager 4 – 6 (96 pages)
	Voyager 5 (160 pages)	5.0 – 6.5	Voyager 5 Workbook	
	Voyager 6 (160 pages)	6.0 – 7.5	Voyager 6 Workbook	
Reading for Work and Life	Voyager 7 (176 pages)	7.0 – 8.5	Voyager 7 Workbook	Teacher's Resource Guide for Voyager 7 and 8 (80 pages)
	Voyager 8 (176 pages)	8.0 – 9.5	Voyager 8 Workbook	

▶ A Closer Look at the Student Books

Voyager contains nine student books.

Foundation Book

The first book is *Foundation Book*. This book has 28 lessons divided into five units. Units 1–3 contain 18 lessons and introduce the sounds and names of single consonants. Unit 4 contains five lessons that introduce the five vowels and the short vowel sounds in a word-family context. Unit 5 contains five lessons introducing common initial consonant blends.

The activities in each lesson give students opportunities to generate words containing the target letters and sounds, and to read and write sentences or stories that contain words with those letters and sounds. The lessons also include activities to build listening, speaking, and critical-thinking skills.

Student Books 1–8

▶ **Units:** Student books 1–8 are each divided into four units organized around themes relevant to adult life, such as Hopes and Dreams, Express Yourself, On the Job, and Resolving Conflict. Each unit contains three lessons in which students explore different aspects of the theme while working with activities that integrate reading, writing, listening, speaking, and thinking skills.

Each unit ends with (1) a one-page Writing Skills Mini-Lesson that teaches a specific writing skill, such as capitalization, and (2) a cumulative unit review that covers the main skills taught in the unit.

▶ **Lessons:** Lessons in student books 1–8 contain the following features:

Pre-Reading Activities: Each lesson begins with a pre-reading activity designed to activate student interest and prior knowledge, or to teach information needed to understand the reading at the heart of the lesson.

Reading Selections: Over the course of the series, students are exposed to a wide variety of authentic, high-quality reading selections. The readings are a rich mixture of short stories; poetry; drama; essays; adult student writings; informational pieces; and common documents, forms, and graphics.

Post-Reading Activities: Through activities related to the reading selection and the unit's theme, students develop their vocabulary, comprehension, and higher-order thinking skills; build their writing competence; and work to master common documents, forms, and graphics. The blend of these features depends on the level of the book.

▶ **Assessment:** Each book begins with a Skills Preview and ends with a cumulative Skills Review. Books 1–6 also contain student self-assessments to use before beginning and after completing each book.

▶ **Answer Key and Reference Handbook:** Students can find an answer key and a reference handbook at the back of each book.

The diagram below shows the organization of Books 1–8.

Organization of *Voyager* Books 1-8

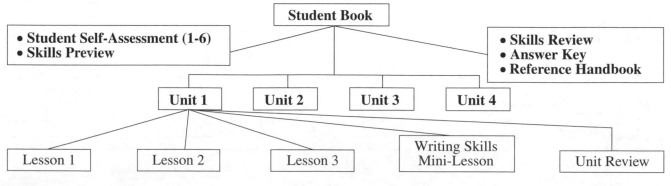

► A Closer Look at Assessment

Assessment in *Voyager* is based on these principles:

1. **Assessment should inform instruction.** Assessment can monitor a student's progress, provide feedback and a framework for remediation, and determine mastery.

2. **Assessment should allow learners to express expectations and evaluate progress.** Specific instruments can help students express their goals and needs and evaluate what they have learned.

3. **Assessment should allow for measurement and documentation of a student's progress and educational gains.** Such documentation is essential for students, teachers, and schools.

Series Assessment Tools

This program provides these assessment tools:

- The **Placement Tool** will help you to place a student in the appropriate *Voyager* student book.
- **Student Interest Inventories** in Books 1–3 and **Student Self-Assessments** in Books 4–6 let students evaluate their level of activity and proficiency with various reading and writing tasks.
- The **Skills Preview** in each student book tests students' proficiency with the reading and writing tasks to be covered in the book.
- **Unit Reviews** test the key skills in the unit.
- The **Skills Review** in each student book tests the key reading and writing skills taught in the entire book.

Alternative Assessment Tools

You can utilize any of the following alternative assessment instruments with *Voyager*.

► Writing

Dialogue Journals: A student writes observations and ideas in a journal on an ongoing basis, and the teacher responds in the journal (see page 12).

Writing Portfolios: These are collections of student writings (see page 12).

► Personal Progress Portfolios

Working Folders: Students date and keep all their works-in-progress and finished work in their working folders. They also keep their "Student Progress Tracking Sheets" in this folder.

Progress Portfolios: Progress Portfolios let students demonstrate progress over time. PCMs have instructions for helping *Voyager* students evaluate the material in their Working Folders and assemble Progress Portfolios.

► Evaluation

Student conferences allow you to evaluate a student's portfolio. These conferences should help students to see their progress as well as show them areas that need improvement. A PCM is provided as a guide for conducting these conferences.

Main Purposes of Voyager Assessment Tools

	Inform Instructor	Empower Learner	Measure Progress
Series Assessments			
Placement Tool	X		
Student Interest Inventory		X	X
Skills Preview	X	X	X
Unit Review	X	X	X
Skills Review	X	X	X
Alternative Assessments			
Dialogue Journal	X	X	
Writing Portfolio	X	X	X
Personal Progress Portfolio	X	X	X

Suggestions for Teaching
Voyager Foundation Book and *Voyager 1*

The first two student books in the *Voyager* series are intended for students at the 0.5–2.5 reading levels. These books assume students have a very basic knowledge of the alphabet and letter/sound correspondences.

▶ Characteristics of Adult New Readers

When working through these or other materials, keep in mind the following characteristics common to adult learners.

Adult learners	As a teacher or tutor of adult learners you should
want and deserve respect but may fear school	• stress accomplishments • give frequent praise • emphasize existing skills
have a wealth of life experience	• emphasize how much students already can do • design some activities around students' interests and experiences
may feel insecure about using new skills	• provide many opportunities for practice • model and practice skills before having students work independently
are accustomed to making decisions	• involve students in setting goals and objectives • offer choices of activities • respect the students' priorities
may find planning for the future difficult	• help students to prioritize learning goals • develop supplemental activities around students' special interests • use time carefully

Adapted from *Teaching Adults: A Literacy Resource Book*, New Readers Press, 1994

▶ Purpose of *Foundation Book* and *Voyager 1*

Voyager Foundation Book emphasizes, within a thematic context, single consonant/sound correspondences, short-vowel word families, and selected two-letter initial blends. Students complete reading and writing tasks while developing a core sight vocabulary and learning basic phonics skills.

Voyager 1 emphasizes some of the key components of the reading and writing processes. Students work on decoding skills, use prereading strategies, and complete postreading comprehension checks. Students also begin to apply higher-order thinking skills, such as making inferences, to their reading, and to follow the key stages of the writing process.

After successfully completing these two books, students will have learned to
- work through theme-based lessons
- decode words with consonant sounds, short and long vowel sounds, consonant blends, and digraphs
- employ a basic sight vocabulary
- utilize several reading strategies
- apply some higher-order reading skills
- take a piece of writing through the writing process
- apply some basic conventions of written English, such as writing sentences and capitalization

▶ Working with Adult New Readers

Voyager has been developed to help adult readers build their reading and writing skills. To accomplish this, adult students should be exposed to a wide variety of written materials in addition to the material in these books. You can also employ a variety of strategies to help adult new readers build their skills and self-confidence. Here are suggestions in four key areas: Word Recognition, Sight Vocabulary, Fluency, and Comprehension.

Improving Word Recognition

When skillful readers come to a word they don't know, they use specific strategies. These strategies need to be taught to readers who don't use them.

1. **Context clues:** Have students try to figure out the meaning of an unfamiliar word by using its context—the surrounding sentence and paragraph. This strategy keeps students focused on the whole piece. Encourage students to try this strategy first when they encounter an unknown word.

   When students come to a word they don't know, have them say "blank" and read the rest of the sentence or paragraph. Have them think of a word that would fit in place of "blank," then reread the sentence using that word to see if it makes sense (even if it isn't correct).

2. **Phonics:** Students can sound out a word using sound/symbol relationships to decode the word. When students come to a word that they can't read, have them underline each consonant and make its sound. Then have them blend the sounds together to make a word and see if the word fits in the context of the sentence. [*"The car was stuck in tr ff c." (traffic)*]

3. **Word families:** All the words in a word family end in the same group of letters and rhyme (*bell, fell, tell, spell*). See page 29, "Working with Word Families," for more information.

Sight Vocabulary

Skillful readers have a body of sight words— words they recognize immediately. The more they read, the more their body of sight words grows.

As students progress, they should build the number of words that they recognize automatically. Students can create flash cards and personal dictionaries with words they encounter frequently and want to learn.

Flash cards: Have students make a card with the target word on the front and either a picture representing the word or a sentence using the word on the back. Have them make cards for 5 to 10 new words at a time. Encourage students to review the words at home. Allow time in each lesson for students to review their cards. As they review, have students divide the cards into two piles—words that they recognize immediately and those they do not. Students can repeat the process until the second pile is gone.

Personal dictionaries: Students can develop their own dictionaries to help them learn sight words. Have them label each page of a notebook with a letter of the alphabet. They can write a word they want to learn and a sentence that uses that word on the appropriate page. Students can also create special pages for different contexts, such as work, school, family, and other topics of special interest.

Increasing Fluency

Many beginning readers read hesitantly and without expression. It is important for them to improve their fluency because it will increase their understanding and enjoyment of written materials. Below are tips for improving reading fluency.

1. **Read aloud:** Read aloud to students while they listen or follow along. The purpose is to model reading with good phrasing and expression.

2. **Echo reading:** Read a sentence aloud and then have students read the same sentence aloud. Gradually increase the amount of text you read.

3. **Paired reading:** You and the students read aloud simultaneously, but you set the pace. As students' fluency increases, lower your voice so that students can clearly hear themselves.

4. **Alternate reading:** Depending on the level of the material and the ability of the student, read the first sentence or paragraph aloud. Then have the student read the next sentence or paragraph. Alternate until you have finished the selection. Students can do this in pairs, but don't pair students who both read hesitantly.

Improving Comprehension

Even if students can read all the words in a selection, they may not understand the meaning of the passage. Research has shown that people get more out of reading if they use strategies that actively engage them in the reading process. Here are strategies to help students improve their comprehension.

1. **Recalling background knowledge:** Have students recall what they already know about the topic of a reading selection. For example, if the selection is about Rosa Parks, ask students what they know about Rosa Parks and her famous bus ride.

2. **Previewing the reading:** Before beginning to read the selection, read its title and discuss any pictures or other graphics.

3. **Setting a purpose:** Either you or the students can set a purpose for reading. You could ask students what they would like to find out— their purpose for reading (*"Find out about Sal's dream."*). When students finish the reading, have them discuss whether they fulfilled this purpose.

4. **Prediction:** When people watch a movie or a TV show, they speculate on what is going to happen as a storyline unfolds. Use the following process to help students apply this to reading. Before reading, discuss the title and any pictures. Have students predict what the selection will be about. While reading, stop periodically and ask questions such as, *"What do you think will happen next?"* or *"How do you think this will end?"* Have students check the accuracy of their predictions as they read. Model this by reading aloud, asking questions, and thinking through your answers aloud.

5. **Retelling:** Students can retell stories to you or to each other. Have them start by saying, *"This story is about . . ."* Have students retell the story in the correct order and include the major points.

6. **Cloze exercises:** These exercises give students practice using context clues to construct meaning. Select a passage that is at or below the student's reading level. Leave the first and last sentence intact. Delete words from the remaining sentences. Be sure to select words for which there is some context. (*"After school, many kids go home to an _____ house,"* rather than *"After _____, many kids go home to an empty house."*) You can also fill in the first letter of the deleted word. (*"After school, many kids go home to an e_____ house."*) Ask students to fill in each missing word and reread each sentence to be sure the word makes sense.

▶ Working with Adult New Writers

Adult students often willingly express their views orally but are hesitant to write them. Here are some strategies to help adult new writers build their writing skills and self-confidence.

As you help students improve their writing, you should
- provide frequent uninterrupted times for writing
- allow more time for actual writing than for writing skills practice
- carry out each writing assignment yourself and share your writing with students

The Writing Process

One key to unlocking the talents of adult new writers is to work with them through the stages of the writing process. Accomplished writers don't simply get an idea, write it down, and produce a final piece. But adult new writers don't know that. They need to be taught that good writing usually involves these five stages.

1. **Prewriting:** deciding what to write about and organizing ideas. To help students generate ideas
   - Write a word or a topic on the board. Have students brainstorm ideas about the topic. Write all of the ideas down; don't dismiss anything. Have students select any ideas they want to use in their writing.
   - Encourage students to organize their thoughts by using simple outlines, lists, or graphic organizers, such as idea maps.
2. **Drafting:** getting ideas down in sentence form. Tell students not to worry about spelling or grammar at this stage. Encourage them to get their ideas down on paper as well as they can, and to ask for help if they need it.
3. **Revising:** clarifying and refining the content. Model how to revise material by asking questions that students should learn to ask themselves. Ask a volunteer to read his or her draft, or read one of your own. Then ask questions such as, *"Have you made the point that you wanted to make? Are the ideas in an order that makes sense? Is there anything you want to add or delete? Have you used the best words?"* Listeners can also give feedback. Based on the responses, the student can revise the draft. As students become better at this process, they can do it in pairs.
4. **Editing:** fixing errors in grammar, mechanics, and usage. When students have revised their drafts to their satisfaction, help them review their work for errors in grammar, spelling, capitalization, and punctuation. Have them use the Reference Handbook in their books. Focus on one or two key concepts at a time so they are not overwhelmed. Look for teachable moments where a specific skill can be practiced.
5. **Publishing:** writing a final draft and sharing it with others. Students can share their work with others in or outside the class. You can display writing in the classroom. Students can make a class book of their writing.

Language Experience Approach (LEA)

This approach is popular with new readers and writers because it uses students' own ideas, experiences, and vocabulary, while allowing the student to concentrate on the composing aspects of writing. Here is one way to conduct a language experience activity.

1. Ask a student to tell you about a recent or important experience.
2. Write down exactly what the student says. Begin each new sentence on a new line. Ask the student to suggest a title.
3. Read the story back to the student and ask for any additions or corrections.
4. Read each sentence to the student, tracking the sentence with your finger. Have the student read each sentence after you.
5. Have the student read the entire story independently. If the student has difficulty, use paired or echo reading (see page 10).

6. Have the student choose words from the story to add to flash cards or to a personal dictionary (see page 9).
7. Have the student copy the story, date it, and place it in a working folder.

Note: When working with a group, have each student contribute one sentence as you write the story on the board.

Journals

Encourage students to keep some type of journal in a notebook. Explain that they don't revise or edit a journal.

- A **personal journal** includes a student's personal thoughts, activities, or observations. Students can keep these private or choose to share them.
- A **dialogue journal** becomes a written dialogue between you and the student. In the journal, you respond to the student's ideas and share your own. You can model corrections in your responses, but do not correct the student's writing.

Handwriting

For adult new writers, handwriting development can be arduous and time-intensive. Here are some ideas to keep in mind.

- Using PCM 1: Letter Formation Chart, show students how to form letters they are unfamiliar with. Choose letters in a student's name or in words that he or she would like to write.
- Don't overdo handwriting practice.
- Students can practice by copying words or sentences that are short and meaningful to them.
- If students can't write in cursive, teach them to sign their names, but don't focus on cursive writing.

Spelling

Students need to understand that while spelling is important in effective writing, becoming a good speller is a long-term process. They need not correct every spelling error in each piece. Take a long-term approach to spelling by following these tips.

- Have students keep a personal spelling list of words that they want or need to know how to spell. Have them label each page of a notebook with a letter of the alphabet. They should write words they want to learn to spell on the appropriate pages. They can also write a sentence that uses the target word if they wish.
- Make lists of words that students commonly use and misspell. Look for patterns in their errors, and teach any rules that relate to the most common mistakes.
- Teach spelling rules that relate to the reading skills you are teaching. For instance, if you are reading the *-ill* word family, explain that the *il* sound is usually spelled *-ill* at the end of words. As with reading, learning to spell a word in a word family gives students the ability to spell other words in that family without having to study each word individually.
- To help students avoid getting bogged down when writing first drafts, encourage them to use **invented spelling**—guessing how to spell a word based on the way it sounds. They can correct their spelling when they edit their work.

Writing Portfolios

For students, one of the most important factors in developing confidence in writing is seeing progress over time. Have students date and keep all their writings in a working folder. Review these writings together periodically and discuss areas of improvement. Students can select special pieces to place in a Writing Portfolio or in a more comprehensive Personal Progress Portfolio (see page 7). Here are some tips for developing either type of portfolio.

- Have students keep unfinished pieces in their working folders.
- Have students use PCM 16 to select the best pieces from their working folders to include in their portfolios.
- If a student takes a piece of work through the writing process, staple the drafts together with the final draft on top. Date the final piece.
- Use PCM 17: Portfolio Conference Questionnaire to help students evaluate their progress.

Foundation Book

▶ *Foundation Book* Scope and Sequence

Foundation Book has five units. All lessons within one unit have the same instructional design. However, the instructional design changes from unit to unit, slowly progressing in difficulty throughout *Foundation Book.*

Unit	Readings	Sight Words	Lesson Objectives
Unit 1: Consonants Lessons 1–5 (b, d, f, h, g, j)	• 1 reading • each sentence on new line	pictures & text	• learn the names and sounds of 6 consonants • identify, dictate, and copy words with the target letters • dictate, copy, and read sentences • learn sight words • read and complete a 3- or 4-line cloze story • dictate, read, and copy a language experience story
Unit 2: More Consonants Lessons 6–12 (c, k, l, m, n, p, q, r)	• 1 reading • each sentence on new line	pictures & text	• learn the names and sounds of 8 consonants • identify, dictate, and copy words with the target letters • dictate, copy, and read sentences • learn sight words • read, complete, and discuss a 5-line cloze story • dictate, read, and copy a language experience story
Unit 3: More Consonants Lessons 13–18 (c, s, t, v, w, y, x, z)	• 1–2 readings • each sentence on new line	pictures & text	• learn the names and sounds of 8 consonants • read and discuss a 4- or 5-line reading • identify, dictate, and copy words with the target letters • learn sight words • read a 7- to 8-line story or poem and add an ending; discuss • dictate, read, and copy a language experience story
Unit 4: Short Vowels Lessons 19–23 (a, e, i, o, u)	• 1 limerick • 1 story • each sentence on new line	text only	• learn the names and short sounds of the 5 vowels • read and discuss a 5-line limerick • generate, read, and write word-family words • learn sight words • read, complete, and discuss a 5- or 6-line cloze story • write sentences • dictate, read, and copy a language experience story
Unit 5: Blends Lessons 24–28 (bl, br, cl, cr, dr, fl, fr, gl, gr, pl, pr, sl, sm, sp, st, sk, sn, tr, tw)	• 2 related stories • paragraph format	text only	• learn the sounds for 19 initial consonant blends • read and discuss a list or a story • generate, read, and write words with the target initial blends • add initial blends to short-vowel word families to make words • learn sight words • read a story • answer comprehension questions about the story • dictate, read, and copy a language experience story

► How to Use *Foundation Book*

You can use *Foundation Book* for one-on-one or small-group instruction. The Teacher's Notes that start on page 16 of this guide provide guidance for teaching each of the lessons in *Foundation Book*. You may adapt these ideas to fit your situation.

Before you begin to work with *Foundation Book*, read "Suggestions for Teaching *Voyager Foundation Book* and *Voyager 1*" on page 8. This material gives insight into the special needs of adult new readers and writers. It suggests specific strategies that have proved successful with adult literacy students.

To begin your work with *Foundation Book*, discuss students' educational goals with them. Describe ways in which you will be helping them reach those goals. Work through the assessment materials at the beginning of the book to assess students' skill levels and needs.

As you work through *Foundation Book*, keep in mind that adult new readers need a lot of feedback. Focus on the positive—what students have learned or accomplished. However, keep in mind that adult students can also detect insincere praise, so be positive but truthful. Encourage as much independence as possible, but be careful not to frustrate students by having unrealistic expectations.

Working with a Range of Students in a Group Setting

If you are involved in group instruction, your students' literacy levels may vary. Students may range from those who are new to reading to those who just need a review before moving on to the next level. It is essential that you get to know your group members as individuals with very specific skill levels and interests.

If students in the group have very diverse skills, you may use any of the following strategies:
- In early lessons, let more advanced students work more independently. Don't let them work ahead of the group, but encourage them to do slightly more work than required by the lesson.

For instance, they may write one or two more sentences than the lesson calls for.
- Continue to have more advanced students do additional work in later units. In Unit 3, they can copy the story in Part 4A, or write sentences based on the story. In Unit 4, they can identify additional word-family words and write additional sentences. In Unit 5, they can write other words with the target blends, or copy the stories.
- If it would be beneficial, pair a more advanced student with another student to work through a lesson. The advanced student might help the other student identify target-letter words or help complete other exercises.

Using the Alphabet (p. 4)

This tool assesses a student's ability to recognize letters of the alphabet and copy them accurately. Work one-on-one as a student completes this page. Ask the student to say the name and sound for each letter. Listen carefully to the pronunciation. Check the way the student copies each letter. Look for signs of common learning disabilities, such as reversing *b*, *d*, *s*, or *z*; making *p*, *b*, *m*, or *w* upside down; or confusing similar letters such as *c* and *o*.

If you find that students have a problem with certain letters, try the following strategies:
- Use PCM 1: Letter Formation Chart to help students form the letters.
- Encourage students to form each letter by starting with the correct stoke. For instance, start a *b* with a downstroke and then add the circle. Reverse the process for *d*: start with the circle and then add the downstroke.
- Help students relate the letter to an object that begins with the letter and resembles the letter's shape (e.g., a snake can look like an *s*).

Using the Skills Preview (p. 6)

The purpose of the Skills Preview is to help you further assess a student's letter and word recognition and copying skills. Work one-on-one as a student completes the preview. You may want to demonstrate how to do the first item in each section, but then let the student work as independently as possible. Ask the student to read the letters, words, and sentences aloud. If he or she has difficulty, read them to the student.

Assess the student's performance on the preview. To be successful in this series, students need to do well on Part A. If students make errors on Part B, examine the types of mistakes they are making—scrambling the order of letters, confusing letters that are similar in formation, inaccurately tracking through words, etc. If students have trouble matching the capital and lowercase letters in Part C, work on handwriting skills. In Part D, look at letter formation, spacing between letters and words, and accurate copying. If patterns of errors emerge in any part of the preview, you will probably need to do extensive one-on-one tutoring as you work through *Foundation Book*.

If a student seems capable of doing higher-level work than required in the preview, you may want to have that student complete the *Foundation Book* Skills Review or the *Voyager 1* Skills Preview to determine if that book is more appropriate.

Working through the Units

For detailed explanations and tips for teaching *Foundation Book* lessons and unit reviews, refer to the Teacher's Notes that begin on page 16.

Each lesson in Units 1 and 2 begins with the section "Talk, Write, and Read." Begin these lessons by following the letter/sound strategy outlined in the notes for Lesson 1. This strategy will help students learn the target letters and the sounds they represent. Although lessons in Units 3–5 follow a slightly different pattern, you can continue to use the same basic strategy to teach the consonants, word families, and consonant blends in those lessons.

Using the Skills Review (p. 86)

The Skills Review is a comprehensive review of the lesson content in *Foundation Book*. Words and characters from throughout the book appear in the Skills Review. Exercise formats in the Skills Review reflect formats in the *Foundation Book* unit reviews. Let students complete the Skills Review as independently as possible. Have them read aloud and explain their answers as they work.

If a student struggles through one or more sections of the Skills Review, assess the area(s) in which the student has trouble. You may want to review lessons and/or units in which these areas are covered. If a student does well on the Skills Review, you should feel comfortable moving that student on to *Voyager 1*.

Using the Reference Handbook (p. 93)

The Reference Handbook contains the following features:
- Numbers
- Months of the Year
- Days of the Week
- *Foundation Book* Word List

You and your students can refer to the Reference Handbook at any time during *Foundation Book* instruction. Here are some tips:
- Sometimes numbers, days, and months will occur naturally in students' dictation. Use those times as opportunities to teach these necessary words and spellings. Refer to the handbook as you do so.
- Use the Reference Handbook to design homework assignments. For example, have students fill in a blank monthly calendar. Have them write the days of the week above the squares and fill in the numbers according to the current month. Students can also copy the numbers, both digits and words, or the months and their abbreviations as homework.
- Encourage students to choose words from the Word List that they want to learn. Students can enter these words on the appropriate pages in their personal dictionaries (see page 9).
- For review and reinforcement, scan the Word List for words from earlier lessons that contain the target letter of the current lesson.

Foundation Book Teacher's Notes

Pre-Assessment

Before you begin Unit 1 with students, be sure to have them complete page 4, "Alphabet," and the Skills Preview (see page 14).

In addition to *Foundation Book,* students will need
- a folder in which to keep their finished work and their work-in-progress (see page 12)
- a spiral-bound or three-ring notebook in which to create a personal dictionary (see page 9)
- another notebook for their personal spelling list (see page 12)

▶ Unit 1: Consonants

Part of Unit	*Foundation Book* pages	TRG pages	Workbook pages
Lesson 1 (B)	8 – 9	16 – 18	4
Lesson 2 (D)	10 – 11	18	5
Lesson 3 (F)	12 – 13	18 – 19	6
Lesson 4 (H)	14 – 15	19	7
Lesson 5 (G and J)	16 – 19	19 – 20	8 – 9
Unit 1 Review	20 – 23	20	10 – 11

Student Objectives

Reading
- Learn the names and sounds of *b, d, f, h, g,* and *j.*
- Identify words with the target letters, using pictures, signs, and own experience.
- Learn sight words.
- Read new words in a series of related sentences and in student-dictated stories.
- Put sentences in sequence.

Writing
- Dictate and copy words with the target letters.
- Dictate and copy sentences.
- Select and copy words to complete sentences.
- Copy student-dictated stories.
- Fill in missing letters to form words.
- Write original sentences using assigned words.
- Complete a crossword puzzle.

Mechanics
- Understand these uses for capital letters: on signs; to begin sentences; for the names of people, months, and days; in titles.

- Understand the purpose of three punctuation marks: period, apostrophe, and question mark.

▶ Unit 1 PCMs
PCM 1: Letter Formation Chart
PCM 2: Student Progress Tracking Sheet
PCM 3: Unit 1 Words

▶ Personal Dictionaries
Encourage students to choose 5 to 10 words to add to their personal dictionaries during each lesson in Unit 1 (see page 9).

▶ Personal Spelling Lists
Encourage students to add words they want to learn to spell to their personal spelling lists (see page 12).

Lesson 1: Bb (pp. 8–9)

Read the lesson title. Point out the capital and lower-case *b* in the alphabets at the top of the lesson pages. Have students say the name of the letter.

1. **Talk, Write, and Read** Read the photo caption. Use the letter/sound strategy outlined below to teach the letter *b.*

A. Talk about what you see in this picture.

1. Discuss the picture on the lesson page. Ask students to describe the scene as a whole.

2. Explain that you will be focusing on words that start with the letter and sound of *b*. Model the sound *b*. Have students repeat the letter and its sound.

3. Ask, *"What objects in the picture start with b?"* Give one or two examples. Point to objects in the picture. Ask students to name the objects. Repeat the words with students.

4. Give one or two examples of objects that have the *b* sound at the end or in the middle. Discuss whether students hear the *b* sound in those positions. Repeat the words with students.

B. Write words with the letter *b* like *book*. You may use words from the picture.

1. Encourage students to say words that contain *b*. The words may include, but should not be limited to, words in the picture.

2. Write the words, underlining each *b*. Read each word aloud. Then have students read the words aloud with you. Finally, let each student read the words aloud independently.

3. Have students copy the words onto the lines in their student book. Also have each student add words they don't know to their personal dictionary (see page 9).

C. Pick one word from your list. Make a sentence with the word. Have students dictate a sentence using one of the words. Write it on the first line; let the student copy it onto the second line.

If you are working with a group of students, have one or more students dictate sentences. Write them on the board. Have students choose a sentence to copy into their books.

D. Read your sentence aloud. Have each student read their sentence aloud at least one time.

▶ **Target words from picture:** *baby, bag, ball, basket, books, book store, boys, bus, by, mailbox*

▶ **What to watch for**

1. When students print the lowercase letter *b*, they might reverse it to look like *d*. If so, point out that the lowercase *b* looks like a capital *B* with the top loop missing.

2. Explain that signs are often written in capital letters (*BOOK STORE*). However, when you write sign words for students to copy, use lowercase letters (*book store*), or write the words both ways.

2. Words to Know Have students read the pictured words with the target letter. Point out the letter *b* and its sound in the initial, middle, and final positions. If students have trouble reading the words, encourage them to use the picture clues.

3. Key Words Explain that these words will be used later in the lesson. Read each word aloud and use it in a sentence.

▶ *Special notes:* Make sure students pronounce the ending of *closed*. Use *closed* and *close* in separate sentences. Mention that *Sunday* begins with a capital letter because it is the name of a day.

4. Read and Write Read the title; ask students to repeat it. Ask, *"What kinds of things can be open and closed?"* Read the words in the word box with students. Help students read each sentence to get a sense of the sentence, saying "blank" for missing words. Then have them read the sentence again, filling in the correct word orally as they read. Have them write the word on the line. Once all sentences are completed, ask students to read them aloud. Point out that each sentence begins with a capital letter and ends with a period.

5. In Your Own Words Have students make up a story about the picture on page 8. Write the story as students dictate it. Have them give it a title. Read the story aloud. Have students read the story aloud and copy it (see "Language Experience Approach" on pages 11–12). Students should date and keep their copies of the story in their working folders.

► **Extensions**

1. Use PCM 1 as a reference to show students how to make each letter. For this lesson, have students practice making *B* and *b*.

2. Encourage students to choose five words they want to learn and to add them to their personal dictionaries and/or make flash cards.

► **More practice:** *Foundation Workbook* p. 4 Make sure students know how to do all the workbook exercises before they begin.

Help students fill out copies of PCM 2 to include in their working folders.

Lesson 2: Dd (pp. 10–11)

Read the lesson title. See Lesson 1 notes.

1. **Talk, Write, and Read** See Lesson 1 notes.

► **Target words from picture:** *December, desk, diploma, dog, Don Adams, door, doorknob, drawers, calendar, window, closed, shade*

► **What to watch for**

1. Students will tend to identify picture words that represent objects. Ask questions to help them identify other words with the target sound (*"Is the book open or closed?" "Is the desk neat or cluttered?"*).

2. If students confuse the lowercase *b* and *d,* point out how the shape of the word *bed* looks like a bed with a headboard and a footboard.

2. **Words to Know** See Lesson 1 notes. Point out target letter *d.*

3. **Key Words** See Lesson 1 notes.

► *Special notes:* Explain that sometimes we use *a* before a word and sometimes *an.* Give examples: *a* book, *a* closed book, *an* open book. Point out that one way is easier to say than the other, depending on the word it precedes. Do not go into further explanation at this point.

4. **Read and Write** Read the title and ask students to repeat it. Explain that *Don* always begins with a capital letter because it is a person's name. Explain the meaning of the possessive

ending *'s* in *Don's.* Ask, *"What kinds of things are found in offices?"* Follow the "Read and Write" process described in Lesson 1. Remind students that each sentence begins with a capital letter and ends with a period.

5. **In Your Own Words** See Lesson 1 notes.

► **Extension:** Give each student a copy of a comic strip or short article. Read it to students. Ask them to underline each *b* or *B* and circle each *d* or *D.* Demonstrate on the board with *December.*

► **More Practice:** *Foundation Workbook* p. 5

Help students fill out copies of PCM 2.

Lesson 3: Ff (pp. 12–13)

Read the lesson title. See Lesson 1 notes.

1. **Talk, Write, and Read** See Lesson 1 notes.

► **Target words from picture:** *fast food, finger, fish, flag, four, Frank, Fred's, french fries, fresh, friends, roof*

► **What to watch for:** Students may suggest words such as *phone* or *laugh* as examples of words with the *f* sound. Explain that some sounds can be spelled in different ways. Write the words for students to see. But ask them to write in their own books only the words that actually have the letter *f.*

2. **Words to Know** See Lesson 1 notes. Point out target letter *f.*

3. **Key Words** See Lesson 1 notes.

► *Special notes:* Demonstrate the meaning of *half* by drawing a circle cut in half. Ask students why *Friday* begins with a capital letter.

4. **Read and Write** Read the title aloud and ask students to repeat it. Ask, *"Why does the word* Frank *begin with a capital letter?"* Then point out other words with capital letters. Explain that main words in titles are capitalized. Ask what Frank and his friends are doing in the picture. See Lesson 1 notes. Be sure students pronounce the final *s* in *eats* ("Frank *eats* half his fish and french fries"). If students tend to drop the final *s* sound when speaking, explain that *eat* differs

from *eats* in both reading and writing. Write and read other examples (*friend drinks coffee/ friends drink coffee; Don works/they work*). Remind students that each sentence begins with a capital letter and ends with a period.

5. **In Your Own Words** See Lesson 1 notes.

▶ **Extension:** Work with students to create a menu. Have them print the names of the foods in the lesson on a piece of paper under the title "Fast Foods." Ask them to suggest prices for each item and help them write the prices.

▶ **More Practice:** *Foundation Workbook* p. 6

Help students fill out copies of PCM 2.

Lesson 4: Hh (pp. 14–15)

Read the lesson title. See Lesson 1 notes.

1. **Talk, Write, and Read** See Lesson 1 notes.

▶ **Target words from picture:** *Hal, hand, hat, his, hood, hose, house, hubcap*

▶ **What to watch for:** Do not ask students to suggest words that end in *h*. In the final position, *h* is either silent (*ah*) or part of a digraph (*cash*).

2. **Words to Know** See Lesson 1 notes. Point out *h* in the initial position.

3. **Key Words** See Lesson 1 notes.

▶ *Special notes:* Be sure students pronounce the final *s* in *puts*. Use *put* and *puts* in separate sentences. Ask students to use each in a sentence.

4. **Read and Write** Read the title; ask students to repeat it. Note the capital letters. Ask, *"Why does the word* Hal *always begin with a capital letter?"* Ask, *"What is Hal doing in the picture?"* See Lesson 1 notes.

5. **In Your Own Words** See Lesson 1 notes.

▶ **Extension:** For each student, cut apart a set of these words beginning with *h* on PCM 3: *has, his, half, He, house, hose, Hal, hand, hold, have.* Students can pair off and use them as flash cards, pasting each word on a card, if they prefer. They could also combine their sets, turn them facedown, and play this memory game: Each player takes

turns turning one card over and then another. If the cards have the same word and the player can read it, he or she keeps the pair and tries again. If the cards do not match, they are turned facedown, and the next player takes a turn. When all the cards are gone, the player with the most pairs wins.

▶ **More Practice:** *Foundation Workbook* p. 7

Help students fill out copies of PCM 2.

Lesson 5: Gg and Jj (pp. 16–19)

Read the lesson title. See Lesson 1 notes.

1. **Talk, Write, and Read** Read the photo caption. Use the letter/sound strategy described in Lesson 1 with two sounds: *g* as in *garden* and *j* as in *jacket* and *giant*.

▶ **Target words from picture:** *g: garage* (first *g*), *garbage can* (first *g*), *garden, gate, gloves, growing, wagon, dig; j: jacket, jeans;* **g as j:** *vegetables, garbage can* (second *g*). Some students may pronounce the second *g* in *garage* as *j*.

▶ **What to watch for:** Focus first on words with the sound *g* as in *garden*. Do exercises 1–5 with students. Then return to the picture and discuss the sound *j* and the two letters that can represent it. If students do not identify words in which *g* sounds like *j*, suggest possibilities (*page, germ, gym*).

2. **G like Garden** Help students select words with this sound from their list. Proceed as usual with sentence dictation.

3. **Words to Know** See Lesson 1 notes. Point out target letter *g* with the sound *g*.

4. **Key Words** See Lesson 1 notes.

▶ *Special notes:* Explain that *May* begins with a capital letter because in the following story it is the name of a month. Discuss a second meaning of *may* and use it in a sentence: *You may read the story now.* See if students can determine that with this meaning, *may* would be capitalized only if it came at the beginning of a sentence or in a title.

5. **Read and Write** Read the title and ask students to repeat it. Read the first sentence. Ask, *"Why*

do the words Jan *and* Gus *begin with capital letters?"* See Lesson 1 notes.

6. **G like Giant** Help students select words with this sound from their list. Proceed as usual with sentence dictation.

7. **J like Jacket** Help students select words with this sound from their list. Proceed as usual with sentence dictation.

8. **In Your Own Words** See Lesson 1 notes.

9. **Words to Know** See Lesson 1 notes. Point out letters *j* and *g* with the sound *j*.

10. **Key Words** See Lesson 1 notes.

▶ *Special notes:* Explain that *July* and *August* begin with capital letters because they are months. Give a sentence to illustrate how *can* will be used in the story: *"I can read the words."*

11. **Read and Write** Repeat the process described earlier in this lesson. Complete one set of sentences before proceeding to the second set.

12. **In Your Own Words** See Lesson 1 notes.

▶ **Extension:** Refer students to "Months of the Year" in the Reference Handbook (*Foundation Book* page 94). Underline the words students have read in Unit 1: *May, July, August, December.* Bring a calendar to class. Have students write their names on their birthdays. Add other important events and review this class calendar regularly.

▶ **More Practice:** *Foundation Workbook* p. 8

Help students fill out copies of PCM 2.

Unit 1 Review (pp. 20–23)

When students have completed Lessons 1–5, have them do this review. Have students read aloud and explain their answers to you when possible, so that you can monitor their progress not only with written work, but also with oral and cognitive work.

1. **Words to Review** Have students say the names and sounds of the consonants. Help them complete the first few words. Let them finish the exercise as independently as possible.

2. **Sentence Pairs** Have students read the words in the word box aloud. Have them read the sentences as independently as possible and choose and write the word to finish each sentence. Finally, have them read their completed sentences aloud, either individually or as a group.

3. **How Do You Know?** Discuss the question mark. Help students read each question. Ask them to pick the more logical answer and to explain their choice.

4. **What's the Order?** Discuss the meaning of sequence. Help students put the first group of sentences into the correct sequence. Have them do the second group on their own. Finally, have them read the sentences aloud and in order. If students have difficulty, print each sentence on a separate card and have students sequence them.

5. **Writing Sentences** Point out that the sample sentence uses all the given words plus several others. Have students dictate sentences B–D. Write the sentences and have students copy them. Have them read the sentences aloud.

6. **Puzzle** Have students read the puzzle words aloud. Help them find the correct location for one or two words. Let students complete the puzzle independently, checking off each word as they use it. If necessary, suggest that they first complete all the horizontal words.

▶ **Extension:** Cut apart the rest of the words in PCM 3. Give each student a set of words that forms a complete sentence. (e.g., *The bank is closed on Sunday.*) Review the words and ask students to make a sentence. Then replace one of the words with another word from the PCM (e.g., replace *bank* with *garage*). Ask students to read the new sentence. Continue replacing words. Tell students to copy the sentence(s). Have them save the cut-up words.

▶ **More Practice:** *Foundation Workbook* p. 10

▶ *Final note:* Review with students the copies of PCM 2 that they completed for this unit. Ask what additional help they think they need. Discuss possible ways of meeting their needs.

▶ Unit 2: More Consonants

Part of Unit	*Foundation Book* pages	TRG pages	Workbook pages
Lesson 6 (C and K)	24 – 25	21 – 22	12 – 13
Lesson 7 (L)	26 – 27	22	14
Lesson 8 (M)	28 – 29	22	15
Lesson 9 (N)	30 – 31	22 – 23	16
Lesson 10 (P)	32 – 33	23	17
Lesson 11 (Q)	34 – 35	23	18
Lesson 12 (R)	36 – 37	23 – 24	19
Unit 2 Review	38 – 41	24	20 – 21

Student Objectives

Reading

- Learn the names and sounds of *c, k, l, m, n, p, q(u),* and *r.*
- Identify words with the target letters, using pictures, signs, and own experience.
- Learn sight words.
- Read new words in a series of related sentences and in student-dictated stories.
- Read with a purpose: to find the answer to a specific question.
- Relate reading content to own experiences.
- Identify homophones (*their, there, they're*).
- Put sentences in sequence.

Writing

- Dictate and copy words with the target letters.
- Dictate and copy sentences.
- Select and copy words to complete sentences.
- Copy student-dictated stories.
- Fill in missing letters to form words.
- Write original sentences using assigned words.
- Complete a crossword puzzle.

Mechanics

- Understand that a question mark indicates a question.
- Understand that holidays are capitalized.
- Understand that a comma signals a pause.

▶ Unit 2 PCMs

PCM 1: Letter Formation Chart
PCM 2: Student Progress Tracking Sheet
PCM 3: Unit 1 Words
PCM 4: Unit 2 Words

▶ Personal Dictionaries and Spelling Lists

Encourage students to add to their personal dictionaries and spelling lists during each lesson.

Lesson 6: Cc and Kk (pp. 24–25)

Read the lesson title. See Lesson 1 notes.

1. **Talk, Write, and Read** See Lesson 1 notes.

▶ **Target words from picture:** *c: cap, coveralls, ice cream cone, cup **k:** keys, kids, bike, parking **ck:** jacket, lock, locksmiths, pickup truck, Vicky*

▶ **What to watch for:** As students say a word for the target sound, write it under the heading *c, k,* or *ck.* If students ask how to tell which spelling the sound *k* has, tell them it usually depends on the letter that comes before or after the sound.

2. **Words to Know** See Lesson 1 notes. Point out the letters *c, k,* and *ck* and the sound *k* in the initial and final positions.

3. **Key Words** See Lesson 1 notes.

▶ *Special notes:* Be sure students pronounce the final *s* on *drives* and *kids.* Give a sentence to illustrate the meaning of *kids* that will be used in the story: "*I have two kids, a boy and a girl.*"

4. **Read and Write** Read the title; ask students to repeat it. Read direction **A** to help students set a purpose for reading. Read the words in the word box with students. Help them read each sentence for the sense of the sentence, filling in the correct word orally as they read. Next have students write the word on the line. When the

story is complete, ask them to read it. Read question **B** and discuss students' answers. Review the use of the question mark.

5. In Your Own Words See Lesson 1 notes.

▶ **Extension:** Help students distinguish between the sounds *g* and *k*. Write the words *garden* and *key*. Read each word and repeat the initial sound. Then say other words (*goat*/*coat*, *gap*/*cap*, *guard*/*card*). Ask students if the new words begin with the sound *g* or *k*. Repeat words that end with *g* or *k* sounds (*rack*/*rag*, *back*/*bag*, *pig*/*pick*).

▶ **More Practice:** *Foundation Workbook* p. 12

Help students fill out copies of PCM 2.

Lesson 7: Ll (pp. 26–27)

Read the lesson title. See Lesson 1 notes.

1. Talk, Write, and Read See Lesson 1 notes.

▶ **Target words from picture:** *Labor Day, ladder, Laundromat, laundry, legs, lightbulb, load, clean, closed, clothes, floor, plant, stool*

▶ **What to watch for:** Students may have difficulty hearing the sound *l* as part of a consonant blend (*clean*). Cover the first letter in *clean*. Ask students to listen to the sound *l* as you read *lean*. Then uncover the *c* and read *clean*, helping students hear that the sound *l* is still there. Students may also have trouble thinking of words that end in *l*. Give them hints such as, *"Is the plant tall or short?"* and *"What is the woman sitting on?"*

2. Words to Know See Lesson 1 notes.

3. Key Words See Lesson 1 notes.

▶ *Special notes:* Ask why *Tuesday* begins with a capital letter.

4. Read and Write Follow the process described in Lesson 6. Explain that *Labor Day* begins with capital letters because it is a holiday.

5. In Your Own Words See Lesson 1 notes.

▶ **Extension:** Use the class calendar you started in Lesson 5. Review the months in order. Have students find Labor Day and circle it. Ask them to select four other holidays, find, and circle them.

▶ **More Practice:** *Foundation Workbook* p. 14

Help students fill out copies of PCM 2.

Lesson 8: Mm (pp. 28–29)

Read the lesson title. See Lesson 1 notes.

1. Talk, Write, and Read See Lesson 1 notes.

▶ **Target words from picture:** *makeup, man, Maria, mirror, money, monster, movies, mustache, Ramon, refreshments, umbrella, woman, arm, restrooms*

▶ **What to watch for:** Students may say the name of the letter *m* instead of its sound. Tell them not to make the sound *m* until their lips are closed.

2. Words to Know See Lesson 1 notes.

3. Key Words See Lesson 1 notes.

▶ *Special note:* Some students have difficulty using *woman* and *women* correctly. Write on the board: <u>a</u> wom<u>a</u>n; <u>some</u> wom<u>e</u>n, and underline the common letters. Use each phrase in a sentence.

4. Read and Write See Lesson 6 notes.

5. In Your Own Words See Lesson 1 notes.

▶ **Extensions**
1. Bring newspaper movie sections to class. Help students identify movies they would like to see. Write the titles for them and have them copy the show times and the theater's phone number.
2. Discuss how telephone numbers are written: area code first, usually enclosed by parentheses; the seven-digit number following. Have students write phone numbers that they know.

▶ **More Practice:** *Foundation Workbook* p. 15

Help students fill out copies of PCM 2.

Lesson 9: Nn (pp. 30–31)

Read the lesson title. See Lesson 1 notes.

1. Talk, Write, and Read See Lesson 1 notes.

▶ **Target words from picture:** *nail, necktie, neighbor, new, newspaper, nine, nineteen, no, noodles, number, nurse, apartment, doorknob, jeans, pants, plant, uniform, man, sign*

▶ **What to watch for:** Help students distinguish between the sound and name of the target letter.

2. Words to Know See Lesson 1 notes.

3. Key Words See Lesson 1 notes.

▶ *Special notes:* Ask students why *Wednesday* begins with a capital letter. Make sure students pronounce the sound *th* in *with*.

4. Read and Write See Lesson 6 notes. Ask students why *Stan* and *Nancy* begin with capital letters. Review the meaning of *'s*.

5. In Your Own Words See Lesson 1 notes.

▶ **Extension:** Work with students to make a list of common "NO" signs (*No Parking, No Smoking, No U-Turn*). Discuss where they might find each sign on the list. Discuss the use of the international symbol for *NO:* ⊘

▶ **More Practice:** *Foundation Workbook* p. 16

Help students fill out copies of PCM 2.

Lesson 10: Pp (pp. 32–33)

Read the lesson title. See Lesson 1 notes.

1. Talk, Write, and Read See Lesson 1 notes.

▶ **Target words from picture:** *pans, pants, Pat's, pears, Pete's Plumbing, picture, pipe, plates, plumber, plunger, pots, problem, open, slippers, mop*

▶ **What to watch for:** Be sure students can distinguish between a possessive (*Pat's*) and a plural (*pots*). Ask them to use each in a sentence.

2. Words to Know See Lesson 1 notes.

3. Key Words See Lesson 1 notes.

▶ *Special notes:* Ask students why *Monday* begins with a capital letter.

4. Read and Write See Lesson 6 notes. Ask why *Pat* begins with a capital letter. Explain that the comma means the reader should pause slightly.

5. In Your Own Words See Lesson 1 notes.

▶ **Extension:** On the current month of the class calendar (see Lesson 5 notes), circle the days students have read so far: Sunday, Monday, Tuesday,

Wednesday, Friday. Ask what small word they all end in (*day*). Make two sets of cards: one set with the name of a day on each card, the other set with their abbreviations. Help students sequence them or match abbreviations to the days.

▶ **More Practice:** *Foundation Workbook* p. 17

Help students fill out copies of PCM 2.

Lesson 11: Qq (pp. 34–35)

Read the lesson title. See Lesson 1 notes.

1. Talk, Write, and Read See Lesson 1 notes.

▶ **Target words from picture:** *quart, queen, quilt, Quinn, quiz, squares*

▶ **What to watch for:** Teach *qu* with the sound *kw*. Explain that *q* is almost always followed by *u*.

2. Words to Know See Lesson 1 notes. Point out *qu* in the initial and middle positions.

3. Key Words See Lesson 1 notes.

▶ *Special notes:* Discuss the different meanings of *show*. Give examples: *"Show me the picture." "Let's watch the TV show."*

4. Read and Write See Lesson 6 notes. Explain that *TV* is short for *television* and is written with capital letters.

5. In Your Own Words See Lesson 1 notes.

▶ **Extension:** Share copies of a TV schedule, in table form, for a weeknight. Explain how the table is set up. Help students find their favorite programs.

▶ **More Practice:** *Foundation Workbook* p. 18

Help students fill out copies of PCM 2.

Lesson 12: Rr (pp. 36–37)

Read the lesson title. See Lesson 1 notes.

1. Talk, Write, and Read See Lesson 1 notes.

▶ **Target words from picture:** *rain, raincoat, rainy, raisin bran, refrigerator, arms, cereal, jars, Florida orange juice, shirt, umbrella, floor, hair, water*

▶ **What to watch for:** Students may have difficulty hearing the sound *r* as part of a consonant blend (*bran*) or with *r*-controlled vowels (*shirt*). If so, focus on words where *r* is easier to hear (*rain*).

2. Words to Know See Lesson 1 notes.

3. Key Words See Lesson 1 notes.

▶ *Special notes:* Write *their, there,* and *they're* for students to see. Explain that the words sound the same, but that they mean different things. Use each in a sentence. Have students do the same.

4. Read and Write See Lesson 6 notes.

5. In Your Own Words See Lesson 1 notes.

▶ **Extension:** Using a newspaper weather section, help students identify and list weather words (*rain, sunny, cloudy*) and their corresponding symbols (slanted lines for rain, a cloud for cloudy). Students can record the weather on the class calendar by drawing the symbol and writing the word.

Explain the meaning of the degree symbol (°) as well as the abbreviations F (Fahrenheit, the temperature scale in the English system) and C (Celsius, the temperature scale in the metric system).

▶ **More Practice:** *Foundation Workbook* p. 19

Help students fill out copies of PCM 2.

Unit 2 Review (pp. 38–41)

When students have completed Lessons 6–12, have them do this review. Have students read aloud and explain their answers to you when possible so that you can monitor their progress not only with written work but also with oral and cognitive work.

1. Words to Review See the Unit 1 Review.

2. Sentence Pairs See the Unit 1 Review.

3. What Do You Think? Read the directions and the first two sentences. Ask students if they think it is a good idea for Ramon and Maria to go to the movies when the garage needs to be

cleaned. Show them how to make a check mark to indicate YES or NO. Have them do B–D as independently as possible. Ask them to explain.

4. What's the Order? See the Unit 1 Review.

5. Writing Sentences Read the first three words aloud and say a sentence that uses all three: *"You must have the key for the truck."* Invite students to think of other sentences. Write one of the sentences for students to see. Have students dictate sentences B–D. Write the sentences and have students copy them. Finally, have them read the sentences aloud.

6. Puzzle See the Unit 1 Review.

▶ **Extensions**

1. Cut apart the words on PCM 4. Help students use these words to make complete sentences. Encourage students to use words cut from PCM 3 as well. Invite students to try to read each other's sentences. Have them save their cut-up words.

2. Conduct a meaning-based categorizing activity using the cut-apart words from PCMs 3 and 4. Create categories, such as days of the week, months, things, action words, buildings, and words related to food or eating. Sort through students' words ahead of time so that they are working only with words that fit into your categories, or let them work with all of the words for a more challenging activity.

Ask students to work in pairs or small groups. Have them separate the words into the appropriate categories. Then, have each pair or group read one category of words aloud to the class.

▶ **More Practice:** *Foundation Workbook* p. 20

▶ *Final note:* Review with students the copies of PCM 2 that they completed for this unit. Ask what additional help they think they need. Discuss possible ways of meeting their needs.

▶ Unit 3: More Consonants

Part of Unit	*Foundation Book* pages	TRG pages	Workbook pages
Lesson 13 (C and S)	42 43	25 – 26	22 – 23
Lesson 14 (T)	44 – 45	26	24
Lesson 15 (V)	46 – 47	26 – 27	25
Lesson 16 (W)	48 – 49	27	26
Lesson 17 (Y)	50 – 51	27 – 28	27
Lesson 18 (X and Z)	52 – 53	28	28
Unit 3 Review	54 – 57	28	29 – 30

Student Objectives

Reading
- Learn the names and sounds of *c, s, t, v, w, y, x,* and *z.*
- Understand that some letters have more than one sound.
- Identify words with the target letters using pictures, signs, and own experience.
- Learn sight words.
- Read new words in the context of short stories, poems, and student-dictated stories.
- Read with a purpose: to find the answer to a specific question.
- Relate reading content to own experiences.
- Identify homophones (*too, to, two; dear, deer*).
- Complete a story.
- Read compound words.
- Make inferences from written material.
- Put sentences in sequence.

Writing
- Dictate and copy words with the target letters.
- Select and copy words to complete sentences.
- Write or copy an ending to a story.
- Copy student-dictated stories.
- Fill in missing letters to form words.
- Write answers to questions.
- Write original sentences using assigned words.
- Complete a crossword puzzle.

Mechanics
- Understand this use for capital letters: names of organizations (teams, businesses).
- Understand the meaning of quotation marks.

▶ **Unit 3 PCMs**
PCM 1: Letter Formation Chart
PCM 2: Student Progress Tracking Sheet
PCMs 3 and 4
PCM 5: Unit 3 Words

▶ **Personal Dictionaries and Spelling Lists**
Encourage students to add to their personal dictionaries and spelling lists during each lesson.

Lesson 13: Cc and Ss (pp. 42–43)

Read the lesson title. See Lesson 1 notes.

1. **Talk and Write** Read the photo caption. Then follow the directions for **A** and **B** on the lesson page. Model the name and sound of each target letter. For **C** you may ask students to select a word from each list and dictate a sentence for each one. Write the sentences and have students copy them on a separate paper.

▶ **Target words from picture:** *s: Sandy, sitting, soda, square, standing, study, glasses, poster, blouse, glass, helps, nurse c: city, Nancy*

▶ **What to watch for:** The letter *s* at the end of a word often has the sound *z,* as in *days.* Explain this to students and ask them to underline each letter with the sound *s* in the words they write.

2. **Words to Know** See Lesson 1 notes. Point out target letters *c* and *s* with the sound *s* in the initial and middle positions.

3. Key Words See Lesson 1 notes.

▶ *Special notes:* Ask students why *June* begins with a capital letter.

4. Read and Write Read direction **A** to help students set a purpose for reading. Explain that *GED* stands for *General Educational Development* and that a person receives the equivalent of a high school diploma upon passing the GED tests. Point to the comma in the story and remind students to pause there. Have students read the story aloud and think of an ending. Have students write it if possible, or write it for them. Discuss question **B**.

5. In Your Own Words See Lesson 1 notes.

▶ **Extension:** Use the "Months of the Year" in the Reference Handbook (*Foundation Book* page 94) to review the names of the months in sequence. Say the names of different months and have students take turns finding them in the class calendar (see Lesson 5). Explain how to write dates using numbers: 12/31/99.

▶ **More Practice:** *Foundation Workbook* p. 22

Help students fill out copies of PCM 2.

Lesson 14: Tt (pp. 44–45)

Read the lesson title. See Lesson 1 notes.

1. Talk, Read, and Write For Part **A**, do steps 1–2 of the letter/sound strategy described in Lesson 1 notes. Then read the story aloud to students. Review the name and purpose of each punctuation mark. When you finish, read the story aloud with students (see page 10). Invite students to read independently. Then complete steps **A.** 3–4 and **B.** 1–3 of the letter/sound strategy. You may want students to dictate sentences using words with the target sound and then copy them in a notebook.

▶ **Target words from picture:** *telephone, tickets, tie, tile, trains, trip, trumpet, trunk, suitcase, coat, hat, state, sweatshirt*

▶ **What to watch for:** Ask students why *September* and *Tony* begin with capital letters. Make sure

students use capital letters only where required when they write.

2. Words to Know See Lesson 1 notes.

3. Key Words See Lesson 1 notes.

▶ *Special notes:* Write *too, to,* and *two* for students to see. Explain that the words sound the same, but that they mean different things. Use each in a sentence. Have students do the same.

4. Read and Write See Lesson 13 notes.

5. In Your Own Words See Lesson 1 notes.

▶ **Extension:** Help students locate their city and state on a map. Explain that the names of cities and states begin with capital letters. Write their city and state on the board and have students copy them. Have students find and write the names of cities and states where families and friends live.

▶ **More Practice:** *Foundation Workbook* p. 24

Help students fill out copies of PCM 2.

Lesson 15: Vv (pp. 46–47)

Read the lesson title. See Lesson 1 notes.

1. Talk, Read, and Write See Lesson 14 notes.

▶ **Target words from picture:** *Valentine card, Valentine's Day, vase, vest, violin, V-neck sweater, oven, stove*

▶ **What to watch for:** Ask students why *Valentine's Day* begins with capital letters. Point out the apostrophe in *Valentine's* and tell students it is there because the holiday is named after St. Valentine.

2. Words to Know See Lesson 1 notes.

3. Key Words See Lesson 1 notes.

▶ *Special notes:* Ask why *February* begins with a capital letter. Explain that the word *I* is always written as a capital letter. Follow the process in Lesson 14 for discussing the homophones *dear* and *deer.*

4. Read and Write Read direction **A** to help students set a purpose for reading. Explain that the valentine is a poem and that the words on the ends of certain lines rhyme. Give examples of rhyming words (*am, ham; dear, near*). Read the poem to students, saying "blank" where words are missing. Have students look at the first stanza. Ask what word(s) they would write in the blank. Tell them that the last word they write should rhyme with *new*. (If they have difficulty, suggest "like you.") Do the same for the second stanza. Explain that the last word should rhyme with *old*. (If necessary, suggest "nice to hold," or "good as gold.") Write the words students choose. Students can copy the words in their books and then read the entire poem. Discuss question **B**.

5. **In Your Own Words** See Lesson 1 notes.

▶ **Extension:** Bring greeting cards with simple rhymes to class. Read each one aloud, omitting a word at the end of one of the lines. Ask students to complete the poems.

▶ **More Practice:** *Foundation Workbook* p. 25

Help students fill out copies of PCM 2.

Lesson 16: Ww (pp. 48–49)

Read the lesson title. See Lesson 1 notes.

1. **Talk, Read, and Write** See Lesson 14 notes.

▶ **Target words from picture:** *wading, walk, water, weeds, wet, woods, swimming*

▶ **What to watch for:** Focus on words with *w* at or near the beginning of the word. If students say a word such as *paw,* write it off to the side and explain that *w* makes a different sound in that word.

2. **Words to Know** See Lesson 1 notes.

3. **Key Words** See Lesson 1 notes.

▶ *Special notes:* Explain that words made by combining two smaller words are called compound words. Write and read the word *sidewalk.* Underline both smaller words and ask students to read them. Do the same with the other compound words that students have read in *Foundation Book: bookstore, newspaper, suitcase.*

4. **Read and Write** Read direction **A** to help students set a purpose for reading. Read the story aloud, saying "blank" for missing words. Reread the story and ask students to suggest words to go in the blanks. Write these words and have students copy them. Have students read the story and discuss question **B**.

5. **In Your Own Words** See Lesson 1 notes.

▶ **Extension:** Help students make a list of their pets. Include the kinds of animals, names, and ages. Talk about why they chose their pets' names.

▶ **More Practice:** *Foundation Workbook* p. 26

Help students fill out copies of PCM 2.

Lesson 17: Yy (pp. 50–51)

Read the lesson title. See Lesson 1 notes.

1. **Talk, Read, and Write** See Lesson 14 notes.

▶ **Target words from picture:** *Yankees, Yo-Yo*

▶ **What to watch for:** If students focus on the sight of *y* and not the sound *y*, they may suggest words such as *party* or *Happy Birthday.* If so, write such words off to the side and explain that *y* makes a different sound in them. Model the sound *y* in *yes* and *year.*

2. **Words to Know** See Lesson 1 notes. Point out target letter *y* in the initial position.

3. **Key Words** See Lesson 1 notes.

▶ *Special notes:* Explain that *birthday* is another compound word. Have students read the whole word and each of its parts. Note the letters *c* and *k* in *cake* and that the sound for each is the same.

4. **Read and Write** See Lesson 16 notes. Point to the quotation marks and explain that they come before and after Wayne's exact words. Have students read the story, answer question **A,** and discuss question **B**.

5. **In Your Own Words** See Lesson 1 notes.

▶ **Extension:** Write the words to "Happy Birthday" and ask students to read them. Have students interview each other and complete this sentence: _____'s *birthday is* _____. Ask them to find this day on the class calendar (see Lesson 5).

▶ **More Practice:** *Foundation Workbook* p. 27

Help students fill out copies of PCM 2.

Lesson 18: Xx and Zz (pp. 52–53)

Read the lesson title. See Lesson 1 notes.

1. **Talk, Read, and Write** See Lesson 14 notes. Explain that *House of Pizza* begins with capital letters because it is the name of a business.

▶ **Target words from picture:** *x: box, exercise, Mexico z: magazines, magazine rack, pizza*

▶ **What to watch for:** Students often confuse the sound and the name of *x*. If students have trouble hearing the sound *x* makes in the example word *exit*, use the word *box*.

2. **Words to Know** See Lesson 1 notes.

3. **Key Words** See Lesson 1 notes.

▶ *Special notes:* If students have difficulty remembering a word, encourage them to look at its shape. Demonstrate by drawing a line around a word to show its shape. Have students do the same with words in their books. For example:

4. **Read and Write** See Lesson 16 notes.

5. **In Your Own Words** See Lesson 1 notes.

▶ **Extension:** Prepare game cards, 4 by 4 squares each. In each square write a letter students have learned. Vary the letters on the cards and distribute them to students. Play a game of BINGO in which you say a sound and students cover the appropriate letter on their cards. The first student to cover four squares in a row wins.

▶ **More Practice:** *Foundation Workbook* p. 28

Help students fill out copies of PCM 2.

Unit 3 Review (pp. 54–57)

When students have completed Lessons 13–18, have them do this review. Have students read aloud and explain their answers to you when possible so that you can monitor their progress not only with written work but also with oral and cognitive work.

1. **Words to Review** See the Unit 1 Review.

2. **Sentence Pairs** See the Unit 1 Review.

3. **How Do You Know?** Read the directions aloud to students. Do **A** together. Have students dictate an answer. Remind them to base their answers on the information in the reading. Write the answer and have students copy it in their books. Have students do **B** as independently as possible. Invite them to share their answers with the rest of the group.

4. **What's the Order?** See the Unit 1 Review.

5. **Writing Sentences** See the Unit 2 Review.

6. **Puzzle** See the Unit 1 Review.

▶ **Extensions**
1. Conduct a meaning-based categorizing activity using the cut-apart words from PCM 5. Create categories, such as months, things, and action words. Follow the process described in Unit 2 Review notes (page 24).

2. Have students use the cut-apart words from PCMs 3, 4, and 5 to make sentences. Have them read their sentences aloud.

▶ **More Practice:** *Foundation Workbook* p. 29

▶ *Final note:* Review with students the copies of PCM 2 that they have completed for this unit. Ask what additional help they think they need. Discuss possible ways of meeting their needs.

▶ Unit 4: Short Vowels

Part of Unit	*Foundation Book* pages	TRG pages	Workbook pages
Lesson 19 (short a)	58 – 59	30 – 31	31
Lesson 20 (short e)	60 – 61	31	32
Lesson 21 (short i)	62 – 63	31 – 32	33
Lesson 22 (short o)	64 – 65	32	34
Lesson 23 (short u)	66 – 67	32 – 33	35
Unit 4 Review	68 – 71	33	36 – 37

Student Objectives

Reading
- Learn the names of the five vowels.
- Learn the short vowel sounds.
- Understand rhyming.
- Read words in word families.
- Generate words that belong to word families.
- Learn sight words.
- Read new words in the context of limericks, short stories, and student-dictated stories.
- Read and evaluate a list of activities.

Writing
- Write word-family words.
- Select and copy words to complete sentences.
- Copy student-dictated stories.
- Write original sentences using assigned words.
- Complete a crossword puzzle.

Mechanics
- Understand the use of the apostrophe in possessive plurals ending in *s.*

▶ Unit 4 PCMs
PCM 1: Letter Formation Chart
PCM 2: Student Progress Tracking Sheet
PCMs 3–5
PCM 6: Unit 4 Words
PCM 8: Letters, Consonant Blends, and Word Families

▶ Personal Dictionaries and Spelling Lists
Encourage students to add to their dictionaries and spelling lists during each lesson.

▶ Explaining Rhyme
Most native speakers of English are familiar with the concept of rhyme. To successfully complete the lessons in Unit 4, students also must be comfortable recognizing and generating rhymes.

Before you begin Unit 4, explain and discuss rhyme—the sound pattern that results when words end with the same sounds. Demonstrate rhyme using one-syllable words, such as *bat, cat, fat, hat.* Let students add to this rhyme pattern. Have students generate rhyme patterns of their own.

▶ Working with Limericks
Each lesson in Unit 4 contains a limerick—a humorous five-line poem. This type of poem is believed to have originated in Limerick, a county of Ireland. In a limerick, the first, second, and fifth lines end with one rhyme, the third and fourth lines end with another rhyme.

Limericks also have an established rhythm pattern. As students read the limericks aloud, have them clap the rhythm, emphasizing stressed syllables and clapping lightly on unstressed syllables.

Explain that limericks are meant to be lighthearted and fun. The limericks in Unit 4 not only describe what is going on in the opening picture, but also provide a chance for students to work and have fun with new words, rhyme, and rhythm.

▶ Working with Word Families
Word families are used for instruction in both Units 4 and 5. Word families are groups of words that end with the same sounds and spellings. All words in a word family rhyme. For instance, the words *bat, cat, hat, sat, flat,* and *that* are all members of the *-at* word family.

When students have a basic sight-word vocabulary, however small, you can use word families to help them build on that vocabulary. Here's how:

1. Choose a word in students' sight-word vocabulary that contains a word family (e.g., *can*). Have students say the word aloud and write it.

2. Ask students to say a word that rhymes with *can*. Be sure the word is in the same word family (it must end with *-an*). Write it under *can*.

3. Ask students to point out the difference between the two words (the initial consonant). Explain that by using a different consonant at the beginning of the word, they have produced a new word. Emphasize that knowing the sound produced by *-an* at the end of a word is a tool to help them read and write new words.

4. Have students read the two words on the list and generate more words to add to the word family. Let students write each new word.

5. When several common words in a word family are listed, stop. Move on to another word family or to another part of the lesson.

Lesson 19: Short a (pp. 58–59)

Explain that the lessons in this unit introduce the five vowels. Name each vowel and have students circle the vowels in the alphabet at the top of the page. Explain that vowels can have many sounds but that in this book, students will work mainly with short vowel sounds.

1. **Talk and Read** Read the directions aloud. Then discuss the picture without focusing on specific words. Explain that the picture relates to the reading selection—a limerick. Explain limericks (see "Working with Limericks" on page 29). Then read the title and the limerick aloud. Talk about rhyming and discuss the limerick's rhyme pattern. Say the words that rhyme (*Pat, cat, hat; jam, ham*). Invite students to think of other words that rhyme. Talk about the rhythm pattern. Read the limerick with students. Then have students read it independently. Have students clap the rhythm as they read.

2. **Word Families** Explain word families (see "Working with Word Families" on page 29).

Use the process described to demonstrate how to create a word family for *-an*. Then read the directions aloud. Say the short *a* word family in the first column (*-at*). Have students repeat it. Then have them read the words in this family. If students have difficulty, have them make the sound for the beginning consonant and the sound for *-at*. Show them how to blend these. Have students think of other words to add to this family. They can use words from the limerick, words from the picture, or other words they know. Write these and have students read them aloud and choose one to write in their books. Work through the other target word families in a similar way. When you finish, say the sound for short *a*. Have students repeat it. Help them hear the sound as you read sample words from the target word families.

▶ **Target word families from picture: *-am:* ham, jam *-at:* cat, fat, hat, Pat**

▶ **What to watch for:** If students suggest a multi-syllable word, such as *cabinet*, when discussing the *-ab* word family, congratulate them and write the word on the side. Explain that the word does include the *-ab* pattern, but because the pattern does not come at the end of the word, the word does not rhyme with the other words and isn't included in the *-ab* family. Do point out that being able to recognize patterns in other places within words will help students to figure out new words. If students have difficulty reading a word with a consonant blend (*crab*), just tell them the sound at this point.

3. **Words to Know** Read each word aloud and use it in a sentence. Have students do the same.

4. **Read and Write** Read the directions aloud. Help students read the words in the word box. Have them read the title and the first sentence of the story aloud. Then have them read each of the sentences for the sense of the sentence, saying "blank" for missing words. Have them read the sentence again, filling in the correct words orally as they read. Ask students to write the correct word on its line. Then have them read the entire story aloud.

▶ **30** *Foundation Book* Teacher's Notes

5. **Writing Sentences** Read the directions aloud. Ask students to think of sentences that include both words in **A** (*I sat in the cab*). Write their sentences and have students read them aloud. They can select one sentence to copy on the line in their books. Do the same for **B**.

6. **In Your Own Words** See Lesson 1 notes.

▶ **Extension:** Have students cut apart the letters of the alphabet and the short *a* word families on PCM 8. Have them combine the consonants with the short *a* word families to create new words. Have students keep the letters and word families in an envelope.

▶ **More Practice:** *Foundation Workbook* p. 31

Help students fill out copies of PCM 2.

Lesson 20: Short e (pp. 60–61)

Read the lesson title. See Lesson 19 notes.

1. **Talk and Read** Discuss the picture without focusing on specific words. Explain that the picture relates to the limerick. Read the title and the limerick aloud. Talk about how it sounds. Discuss why Sandy had trouble spelling *cell*. Then read the limerick with students. Finally, have them read it aloud independently.

2. **Word Families** Say the short *e* word family in the first column (*-ed*). Have students repeat it. Then have them read the words in this family. If students have difficulty, have them make the sound for the beginning consonant and the sound for *-ed*. Show them how to blend these. Have students think of other words to add to this family. They can use words from the limerick, words from the picture, or other words they know. Write these and then have students read them aloud and choose one to write in their books. Work through the other target word families in a similar way. When you finish, say the sound for short *e*. Have students repeat it. Help them hear the sound as you read sample words from the word families.

▶ **Target word families from picture:** *-ell: spell* *-ess: dress*

▶ **What to watch for:** Students may suggest verbs that have the verb ending *-ed* as examples of the *-ed* word family. This ending can have three different sounds: *t* as in *kicked*, *d* as in *obeyed*, and *id* as in *parted*. Students might suggest other words that have the short *e* sound (*when, desk*) but do not belong to the word families listed in this section. If so, write them on the board. Congratulate students on their ability to recognize the short *e* sound in other words, but do not try to teach more than the four new patterns at this time. Suggest that students add those words to their personal dictionaries.

3. **Words to Know** See Lesson 19 notes.

▶ *Special note:* Make sure students pronounce *-ing* at the end of *learning*. Have them suggest other words with this ending and give a sentence for each.

4. **Read and Write** See Lesson 19 notes.

▶ *Special note:* Write the words *pets* and *pets'*. Ask what is different about them ('). Have students find the word *pets'* in the story. Explain that the apostrophe means that the messy beds belong to all the pets. You do not have to add *s* with the apostrophe because the word already ends in *s*.

5. **Writing Sentences** See Lesson 19 notes.

6. **In Your Own Words** See Lesson 1 notes.

▶ **Extensions**
1. Write two-line rhymes, leaving out the last word in one. (*My cat's name is Ted. / He lives in the ____.*) Read the two lines aloud. Have students fill in the missing word and then read the two lines.
2. Have students cut out the short *e* word families from PCM 8 and use them with the consonants they cut out for Lesson 19 to build new words.

▶ **More Practice:** *Foundation Workbook* p. 32

Help students fill out copies of PCM 2.

Lesson 21: Short i (pp. 62–63)

Read the lesson title. See Lesson 19 notes.

1. **Talk and Read** See Lesson 20 notes.

2. Word Families See Lesson 20 notes.

▶ **Target word families from picture:** *-ick: pick -ill: grill -it: sit -ip: chip, dip*

▶ **What to watch for:** Students may suggest *Vicky* for the *-ick* word family. Explain that *Vicky* contains the *-ick* pattern but does not belong in the *-ick* word family because the pattern is not at the end of the word. Remind them that being able to recognize patterns in words will help them figure out new words.

3. Words to Know See Lesson 19 notes.

▶ *Special note:* Use *cooks* in a sentence as a verb, as in the story. (*My son cooks dinner on Wednesdays.*)

4. Read and Write See Lesson 19 notes.

5. Writing Sentences See Lesson 19 notes.

6. In Your Own Words See Lesson 1 notes.

▶ **Extensions**

1. Explain that one word can have many different meanings. Use *cook* as an example: *good cook, cook dinner, cook up an excuse, cook his goose.* Help students find other words in the lesson that can have more than one meaning (e.g., *pick, bill, chip, bit*).

2. Have students use their cut-up consonants from PCM 8 and the four short *i* word families to build new words.

▶ **More Practice:** *Foundation Workbook* p. 33

Help students fill out copies of PCM 2.

Lesson 22: Short o (pp. 64–65)

Read the lesson title. See Lesson 19 notes.

1. Talk and Read See Lesson 20 notes.

2. Word Families See Lesson 20 notes.

▶ **Target word families from picture:** *-ock: rock -og: dog, fog, jog -op: top*

▶ **What to watch for:** The sound of *o* in the pattern *-og* varies, especially regionally. For instance, in some areas, *fog* will rhyme with *jog* but not with *dog* or *log*. Tell students it is all right to use the

pronunciations they are used to. The important thing is that they recognize the word family in new words.

3. Words to Know See Lesson 19 notes.

▶ *Special notes:* Write the words *do* and *does*. Use each one in a sentence. (*Mary does her laundry. Mary and Jim do their laundry.*) Have students give sentences for each one.

4. Read and Write See Lesson 19 notes. Remind students to pause when they come to a comma.

5. Writing Sentences See Lesson 19 notes.

6. In Your Own Words See Lesson 1 notes.

▶ **Extensions**

1. Create a list of things students do for exercise. Ask how many students do each activity. Write the number next to each item. Have students copy the list, putting the items in order from most popular to least popular.

2. Have students use their cut-up consonants from PCM 8 and the four short *o* word families to build new words.

▶ **More Practice:** *Foundation Workbook* p. 34

Help students fill out copies of PCM 2.

Lesson 23: Short u (pp. 66–67)

Read the lesson title. See Lesson 19 notes.

1. Talk and Read See Lesson 20 notes. Call attention to the possessive ending on *Gus's*.

2. Word Families See Lesson 20 notes.

▶ **Target word families from picture:** *-ub: sub -uff: cuff -ug: jug, plug*

▶ **What to watch for:** If students suggest words such as *rough* when discussing the *-uff* word family, write the words to the side. Explain that they do rhyme with words in the family, but that you won't include them in the family because the spelling is different.

3. Words to Know See Lesson 19 notes.

▶ *Special notes:* Ask students why *January* begins with a capital letter. If students question the sounds and spellings of the digraphs *ch* and *sh*, tell them these are special sounds they will learn about in *Voyager 1.*

4. Read and Write See Lesson 19 notes.

5. Writing Sentences See Lesson 19 notes.

6. In Your Own Words See Lesson 1 notes.

▶ **Extensions**

1. Share copies of the Food Guide Pyramid developed by the U.S. government. Read the names of the food groups and the recommended number of daily servings for each group. Work with students to generate a list of foods that would meet these recommendations for one day.

2. Have students use their cut-up consonants from PCM 8 and the four short *u* word families to build new words.

▶ **More Practice:** *Foundation Workbook* p. 35

Help students fill out copies of PCM 2.

Unit 4 Review (pp. 68–71)

When students have completed Lessons 19–23, have them do this review. Have students read aloud and explain their answers to you when possible so that you can monitor their progress not only with written work but also with oral and cognitive work.

1. Sentence Pairs See the Unit 1 Review.

2. Word Families Read the directions aloud. Have students work independently to add one word to each word family. When they finish, have students say the ending pattern and read the words in each family. Check their spelling.

3. Make Words Read the directions aloud. Have students read the example words in list **A:** *lab, let, lip, log, lug.* Then ask them to make words the same way for **B–E** and read them aloud.

4. What Do You Want to Do? Read the directions aloud. Read each choice aloud and ask students to check the activities they want to do. Then have them read the items they checked and discuss the reasons for their choices.

5. Writing Sentences See the Unit 2 Review.

6. Puzzle See the Unit 1 Review.

▶ **Extensions**

1. Cut apart the words on PCM 6. Give each student several words. Ask them to pick two of the words and write a sentence with each. Remind them to use capital letters and periods where needed. Have students read their sentences aloud. Correct spelling or grammar only if students ask you to. Have students keep the words in an envelope.

2. Conduct a meaning-based categorizing activity using the cut-apart words from PCM 6. Create categories, such as things, action words, and time words (e.g., *soon, until, when*). Follow the process described in Unit 2 Review notes (page 24).

3. Have students use the cut-apart words from PCMs 3, 4, 5, and 6 to make sentences. Have them read their completed sentences aloud.

▶ **More Practice:** *Foundation Workbook* p. 36

▶ *Final note:* Review with students the copies of PCM 2 that they have completed for this unit. Ask what additional help they think they need. Discuss possible ways of meeting their needs.

▶ Unit 5: Blends

Part of Unit	*Foundation Book* pages	TRG pages	Workbook pages
Lesson 24 (bl, br, cl, cr)	72 – 73	34 – 35	38
Lesson 25 (dr, fl, fr)	74 – 75	35	39
Lesson 26 (gl, gr, pl, pr)	76 – 77	36	40
Lesson 27 (sl, sm, sp, st)	78 – 79	36	41
Lesson 28 (sk, sn, tr, tw)	80 – 81	36 – 37	42
Unit 5 Review	82 – 85	37	43 – 44

Student Objectives

Reading
- Learn to produce the sounds for 19 initial blends.
- Read and generate words with the blends.
- Create new words by adding consonant blends to short-vowel word families.
- Learn sight words.
- Read new words in the context of lists, stories in paragraph form, and student-dictated stories.
- Read with a purpose: to find the answer to a specific question or to make a prediction.
- Make inferences from written material.
- Use story details to support answers.
- Read and evaluate a list of activities.

Writing
- Copy student-dictated stories.
- Select and copy words to complete sentences.
- Write original sentences using assigned words.
- Complete a crossword puzzle.

Mechanics
- Understand the meaning of an ampersand (&), an exclamation point (!), and a hyphen (-).

▶ Unit 5 PCMs
PCM 1: Letter Formation Chart
PCM 2: Student Progress Tracking Sheet
PCMs 3–6
PCM 7: Unit 5 Words
PCM 8: Letters, Consonant Blends, and Word Families

▶ Personal Dictionaries and Spelling Lists
Encourage students to set up a separate page in their dictionaries for each blend covered in Unit 5.

Lesson 24: B & C Blends (pp. 72–73)

Explain that the lessons in this unit focus on consonant blends. All the blends in this unit have two letters and come at the beginning of words. Explain that you can hear both sounds in each blend. Have students look at the lesson title. Tell them that the blends in Lesson 24 will begin with *b* or *c*. Explain that the ampersand (&) means *and*.

1. **Talk and Read** Read the directions aloud. Discuss the picture without focusing on specific words. Read "Quinn's Rules" aloud. Have students discuss why Quinn needs these rules. Read the list again with students. Finally, have students read the list independently.

2. **Blends** Read the directions aloud. Explain that we hear the sound for each letter, but the sounds are close together. Say the sound *bl*. Have students repeat the sound. Read the list of words that start with *bl*. Have students do the same. Ask students to think of other words that begin with *bl*. They can use words from the reading, words from the picture, or other words they know. Write the words and have students read them aloud and choose one to write in their books. Work through the other three blends the same way. Have students add to their personal dictionary pages for each blend.

▶ **Target blends from picture:** *bl: black, blouse cl: clean, clothes, clutter br: broom*

▶ **What to watch for:** Discourage students from adding a vowel sound in the middle of a blend (e.g., "bu-les" for *bless;* "bu-ring" for *bring*). The vowel sound will make it harder to decode words.

3. **Make Words** Read the directions aloud. Have students say the sounds for the four blends. Then have them say the sound for the word family in the first column (*-ab*). Model how to put the first blend (*bl*) together with this word family to form a word (*blab*). Ask students if this is a real word. If they say yes, have them use it in a sentence. Do the same with the other three blends and the *-ab* family. Have students write two of the blends that form real words with *-ab* on the lines in column 1. Do this with the remaining word families. When students finish, have them read their words.

4. **Words to Know** See Lesson 19 notes.

▶ *Special notes:* Ask which words start with more than one consonant (*spill, sweep*). Point out that *sp* and *sw* are also consonant blends.

5. **Read and Think** Read the directions aloud. Explain that the story tells more about how Quinn and her children clean the house. Read the story to students, then read it with them. Finally, have students read independently. Read direction **A.** Ask students to check the title they think best fits this story and write it on the line. Have them read their answers aloud and explain their choices. Read each of the remaining questions and have students mark their answers. Tell them to use only the information in the story to answer the questions.

6. **In Your Own Words** See Lesson 1 notes.

▶ **Extension:** To provide extra practice reading and spelling words with blends, make a white flash card with the following short-vowel pattern: *-ash*. On three colored cards, write the following letters: *c, r,* and *cr*. Have students place each colored card in front of the white card and read the new word. Do the same with the following: *ed, b, l, bl; ag, b, r, br; ap, c, l, cl; og, c, l, cl.*

▶ **More Practice:** *Foundation Workbook* p. 38

Help students fill out copies of PCM 2.

Lesson 25: D & F Blends (pp. 74–75)

Read the lesson title and blends. Have students repeat the blends.

1. **Talk and Read** Read the directions aloud and discuss the picture. Read the story aloud. Have students discuss what they found out. Then read the story again, with students. Finally, invite students to read it independently.

2. **Blends** See Lesson 24 notes.

▶ **Target blends from picture:** *dr: driver, drop fl: flipped, floor, florist, flowers fr: Frank, fresh*

▶ **What to watch for:** Students have not yet studied the vowel sounds in words such as *floor* and *flower*. If they cannot read them, simply tell them what the words are.

3. **Make Words** See Lesson 24 notes. Use the blends shown. Tell students the sound of any word family they have not studied (*-esh*).

4. **Words to Know** See Lesson 19 notes.

▶ *Special note:* Some students may pronounce *holds* and *holes* the same way. Write both words. Say each one and use it in a sentence. Ask students to do the same.

5. **Read and Think** See Lesson 24 notes. Note that C requires only an oral response.

6. **In Your Own Words** See Lesson 1 notes.

▶ **Extensions**
1. Have students measure the size of people and objects in the classroom with rulers and yardsticks. Show how to write feet and inches (*6'4"*) and teach the sight words *height, width,* and *length.*
2. Have students use these cut-up letters and letter groups from PCM 8 to make words: *d, f, l, r, dr, fl, fr, esh, ip, op, og, ug.*

▶ **More Practice:** *Foundation Workbook* p. 39

Help students fill out copies of PCM 2.

Lesson 26: G & P Blends (pp. 76–77)

Read the lesson title and blends. Have students repeat the blends.

1. Talk and Read See Lesson 25 notes.

2. Blends See Lesson 24 notes.

▶ **Target blends from picture:** *gl: glad pl: diploma gr: congratulations, graduation pr: present, proud*

▶ **What to watch for:** Be sure students know one meaning for each word listed. Check by asking them to use the words in a sentence.

3. Make Words See Lesson 24 notes.

4. Words to Know See Lesson 19 notes.

▶ *Special notes:* Ask students why *April* begins with a capital letter.

5. Read and Think See Lesson 24 notes.

6. In Your Own Words See Lesson 1 notes.

▶ **Extensions**

1. Review the lists of the months and days in the Reference Handbook. Make sure each student can say the months in order. Make a list of holidays. Have students match each holiday with its month and use the class calendar to check the answers.

2. Have students use these cut-up letters and letter groups from PCM 8 to make words: *g, l, p, r, gl, gr, pl, pr, ass, and, op, oom, ip, ab.*

▶ **More Practice:** *Foundation Workbook* p. 40

Help students fill out copies of PCM 2.

Lesson 27: S Blends (pp. 78–79)

Read the lesson title and blends. Have students repeat the blends.

1. Talk and Read See Lesson 25 notes. Ask students what they think will happen next, and why.

2. Blends See Lesson 24 notes.

▶ **Target blends from picture:** *sl: sleeve, slice sp: spaghetti, spoon sm: smile st: Stan, steam, stir, stove*

▶ **What to watch for:** Students may have difficulty with the meanings of *slope* and *smog*. Ask students to use the words in sentences.

3. Make Words See Lesson 24 notes.

4. Words to Know See Lesson 19 notes.

▶ *Special notes:* Write *of* and *off*. Read each word aloud and use it in a sentence. Have students do the same.

5. Read and Think See Lesson 24 notes. Discuss the predictions students made in Part 1. Explain the use of the exclamation point (!).

6. In Your Own Words See Lesson 1 notes.

▶ **Extensions**

1. Copy the directions for cooking pasta from a product box. Give a copy to each student. Read the directions aloud and discuss them. Use measuring cups and spoons to help explain words like *quart* and *teaspoon.*

2. Have students use these cut-up letters and letter groups from PCM 8 to make words: *s, m, l, p, t, sm, sl, sp, st, ell, ill, ick, op.*

▶ **More Practice:** *Foundation Workbook* p. 41

Help students fill out copies of PCM 2.

Lesson 28: S & T Blends (pp. 80–81)

Read the lesson title and blends. Have students repeat the blends.

1. Talk and Read See Lesson 25 notes. Point out the hyphens in *twenty-five* and *twenty-two.* Explain that a hyphen is used to join number words from *twenty-one* through *ninety-nine.*

2. Blends See Lesson 24 notes.

▶ **Target blends from picture:** *sk: skates, skis sn: snow tr: tree, try*

▶ **What to watch for:** If students say words with the blends *sc* (*scab*) or *sch* (*school*), write the words in a separate list. Explain that the sound *sk* can be spelled different ways. Help students think of words that use *sk*. Ask, *"What's the name of the small black animal with a white stripe on its back?"*

3. Make Words See Lesson 24 notes.

4. Words to Know See Lesson 19 notes.

▶ *Special notes:* Write *try* and *tries*. Read each word aloud and use it in a sentence. Have students do the same. Repeat with *fry* and *fries*.

5. Read and Think See Lesson 24 notes.

6. In Your Own Words See Lesson 1 notes.

▶ **Extensions**

1. Have students reread one of the stories they dictated previously. Have them suggest titles. Write the titles and ask students to choose the best one. Have them explain their choice. Do the same with other dictated stories or news articles.

2. Have students use these cut-up letters and letter groups from PCM 8 to make words: *s, t, k, n, r, w, sk, sn, tr, tw, ack, im, in, uck.*

▶ **More Practice:** *Foundation Workbook* p. 42

Help students fill out copies of PCM 2.

Unit 5 Review (pp. 82–85)

When students have completed Lessons 24–28, have them do this review. Have students read aloud and explain their answers to you when possible so that you can monitor their progress not only with written work but also with oral and cognitive work.

1. Sentence Pairs See the Unit 1 Review, Part 2.

2. Make Words Read the directions aloud. Have students do the activity independently. Then have them read their words aloud. If students give an answer that is not a real word or seem unsure of the meaning of a word, ask them to use it in a sentence.

3. What Do You Want to Do? See the Unit 4 Review, Part 4.

4. How Do You Know? Read the directions aloud. Have students read the stories and answer the questions as independently as possible. They should write complete sentences (see examples in the Answer Key).

5. Writing Sentences See the Unit 2 Review. If students have trouble, give this example for number 1: *Do not drop crumbs on the floor.*

6. Puzzle See the Unit 1 Review.

▶ **Extensions**

1. Cut apart the words on PCM 7. Explain that many listings are arranged in alphabetical order. Mention dictionaries, telephone directories, and the Word List in the back of their book. Give each student four words from *Foundation Book* that begin with different letters. Help them put the words in alphabetical order. Have them check each other's work, then repeat the activity with different words.

2. Conduct a meaning-based categorizing activity using the Word List on pages 95 and 96 of the student book. Create categories, such as things to cat, places to go, names that are capitalized, etc. Follow the process described in Unit 2 Review notes (page 24).

3. Have students use some of the cut-apart words from PCMs 3, 4, 5, 6, and 7 to make sentences. Have them read their sentences aloud.

▶ **More Practice:** *Foundation Workbook* p. 43

▶ *Final note:* Review with students the copies of PCM 2 that they have completed for this unit. Ask what additional help they think they need. Discuss possible ways of meeting their needs.

Skills Review (pp. 86–88)

When students have completed Unit 5, have them complete the Skills Review (see "Using the Skills Review" on page 15).

▶ **Final Assessment:** Schedule a meeting with each student to go over the material in their working folders. At the conference, discuss the progress shown by the material in the folders. Although they are intended for use with *Voyager 1,* you can refer to PCMs 16 and 17 for guidelines.

Voyager 1

▶ Voyager 1 Scope and Sequence

Voyager 1 is intended for students reading at the 1.0–2.5 reading levels.

Unit	Part of Unit	Reading Selection	Genre	Reading Strategy
Unit 1: Hopes and Dreams	Lesson 1	A Class of Hopes	Story	Use prior experience
	Lesson 2	A New Life	Story	Build on background knowledge
	Lesson 3	Dreams	Poetry	Visualize what you read
	Writing Skills Mini-Lesson			
	Unit 1 Review			
Unit 2: Everyday Heroes	Lesson 4	A Bus Ride	Historical account	Build on background knowledge
	Lesson 5	Neighbor Saves Family	News article	Visualize what you read
	Lesson 6	Can't	Poetry	Use prior experience
	Writing Skills Mini-Lesson			
	Unit 2 Review			
Unit 3: Thrilling Moments	Lesson 7	The Promotion	Story	Use prior experience
	Lesson 8	The Thrill of the Race	Story	Build on background knowledge
	Lesson 9	Winner	Poetry	Visualize what you read
	Writing Skills Mini-Lesson			
	Unit 3 Review			
Unit 4: Friendship	Lesson 10	The Arch	Poetry	Build on background knowledge
	Lesson 11	A Special Friend	Poetry	Use prior experience
	Lesson 12	Sophia's Journal	Journal entry	Visualize what you read
	Writing Skills Mini-Lesson			
	Unit 4 Review			

Reading and Thinking Skill	Writing	Speaking and Listening	Word Work	TRG pages	Workbook pages
Sequence events	Make a list	Discussion	Short vowels (*a, e, i, o, u*)	43 – 45	4 – 5
Identify cause and effect	Write a poem	Retell	Initial consonant blends (*br, cl, gr, pl, st*)	45 – 46	6 – 7
Understand the main idea	Write a poem	Discussion	Final consonant blends (*ft, ld, mp, nt, st*)	46 – 47	8 – 9
	Sentences and capitalization			47	10 – 11
				47	12 – 13
Make predictions	Write about a reading	Retell	Long *a* and long *i*	48 – 49	14 – 15
Find details	Write about a person you interview	Oral reading/ discussion	Long *e* and long *y*	50 – 51	16 – 17
Make inferences	Write a paragraph	Oral reading/ discussion	Long *o* and long *u*	51 – 52	18 – 19
	Contractions			52	20 – 21
				52	22 – 23
Identify cause and effect	Write a story	Discussion	Digraphs (*sh, ch, th, ph, wh*)	53 – 54	24 – 25
Sequence events	Make a list	Retell	3-letter initial blends (*scr, spl, spr, str, thr*)	54 – 56	26 – 27
Make inferences	Write a poem	Oral reading/ discussion	3-letter final blends (*nch, nce, nge, rse, dge*)	56 – 57	28 – 29
	Plurals			57	30 – 31
				57	32 – 33
Understand the main idea	Write a poem	Oral reading/ discussion	Special vowel combinations (*au, aw, oi, oy, oo, ou*)	58 – 59	34 – 35
Find details	Complete a diagram	Oral reading/ discussion	*R*-controlled vowels (*are, err, ire, ore, ure*)	59 – 60	36 – 37
Make predictions	Make a journal entry	Retell	More *r*-controlled vowels (*ar, er, ear, our*)	60 – 61	38 – 39
	Add -*ed* and -*ing*			62	40 – 41
				62	42 – 44

▶ Overview of Voyager 1

Parts of the Book

The Four Units

Below is a short explanation of the unit features in *Voyager 1*. Detailed explanations and tips for teaching the lessons, mini-lessons, and reviews are given in the Teacher's Notes that start on page 43.

▶ **Unit Overviews:** Each unit overview introduces the theme of the unit. Throughout the unit, students will work with readings and activities related to this theme.

▶ **Lessons:** Each unit has three lessons. Each lesson contains the following features:

Learning Goals: a list of the main objectives of each lesson section. Knowing the goals for study empowers students to take charge of the learning process.

Before You Read: a strategy to help students prepare for and better understand the reading selection. Students are encouraged to think about their own knowledge of or experience with the reading topic, or they are given essential background information.

Key Words: words in the lesson that students may not recognize or know the meaning of, presented in meaningful context

As You Read: a reminder to help students apply the reading strategy

Reading: a story, poem, article, or journal entry relating to the theme of the unit

After You Read: questions and activities to check students' comprehension of and reaction to the reading selection

Think About It: instruction and guided practice in a targeted reading and thinking skill

Write About It: instruction and guided practice in a given type of writing, such as a list or a poem

Word Work: introduction of word-attack strategies and phonics skills to help students better decode and write words. Practice is included.

Update: a feature that allows students to revisit a story, providing closure to the lesson

▶ **Writing Skills Mini-Lessons:** These one-page mini-lessons appear at the end of each unit. They feature a particular issue of mechanics or sentence structure that will help students master some basic conventions of written English.

▶ **Unit Reviews:** The unit reviews are cumulative reviews of the reading, writing, and word work activities in each unit. The writing process is introduced and practiced.

Before Starting the Units

▶ **Student Interest Inventory:** This assessment tool lets students evaluate their current level of activity and proficiency with a variety of everyday reading and writing tasks. You will need to work through it individually with students.

▶ **Skills Preview:** The Skills Preview helps you diagnose how well students read independently.

While Working through the Units

▶ **Answer Key:** The Answer Key provides answers to exercises in the lessons, unit reviews, and Writing Skills Mini-Lessons.

▶ **Reference Handbook:** You and your students can refer to the handbook at any time during *Voyager 1* instruction.

After Working through the Units

▶ **Skills Review:** The Skills Review is a cumulative review of the skills taught in *Voyager 1*.

If students did well on the Skills Review, you should feel comfortable moving them on to *Voyager 2*.

▶ How to Use *Voyager 1*

You can use *Voyager 1* for one-on-one or group instruction. The Teacher's Notes that start on page 43 will guide you through each lesson in *Voyager 1*. You may adapt these notes to fit your needs.

Before you begin to work with *Voyager 1*, read "Suggestions for Teaching *Foundation Book* and *Voyager 1*" on page 8. This material gives insight into the special needs of adult new readers and writers. It suggests specific strategies that have proved successful with adult literacy students.

To begin your work with *Voyager 1*, discuss students' educational goals with them. Describe ways in which you will be helping them reach those goals. Work through the assessment materials at the beginning of the book to assess students' skill levels and needs.

As you work through *Voyager 1* with students, assess what material each student can do independently and on what type of material he or she needs guidance. Encourage as much independence as possible, but be careful not to frustrate students by having unrealistic expectations.

Adult new readers need a lot of feedback. Focus on the positive—what students have learned or accomplished. However, keep in mind that adult students can also detect insincere praise, so be positive, but truthful.

Working with a Range of Students in a Group Setting

If you are involved in group instruction, your students' literacy levels may vary. Students may range from those who are new to reading to those who just need a review before moving on to *Voyager 2*. It is essential that you get to know your group members as individuals with very specific interests and skill levels.

Although students may be placed in a class based on their assessed reading level, you will find that adult new readers have diverse skills and skill levels. The following strategies can be used with a mixed-ability group:

- Work through the first unit of *Voyager 1* with the entire class. If some students move quickly through the material on their own, let those students work ahead in a lesson independently, drawing them back in for whole-group discussions and peer review of writing assignments.
- Involve the more able students in peer tutoring. For instance, have students read to each other and review each other's work.
- The more able students can do reinforcement and extension activities while the rest of the class finishes a lesson. They can complete the workbook pages or the extension activities suggested in the Teacher's Notes.

Using the Student Interest Inventory (p. 6)

Before doing the inventory, explain that it will help you get to know the student better and will give the student a way to evaluate his or her progress over time. Explain that the student will fill in the left side of the chart now, and the right side after finishing *Voyager 1*.

Have the student try to read and fill in the first question independently. If necessary, read it aloud and fill in the student's dictated answer.

For parts **B** and **C**, you or the student should read the central column. Have the student check the appropriate answer on the left side of the chart.

Using the Skills Preview (p. 8)

Work one-on-one with a student to complete the preview. Read the directions to each section aloud, then have the student complete the section as independently as possible.

Use the Skills Preview Answers and the Skills Chart to get a sense of the student's comfort level with material taught in *Voyager 1*. Discuss the results with the student. If a student has great difficulty with the Skills Preview, consider moving the student to the *Voyager Foundation Book*.

Conversely, if a student completes the preview with little or no difficulty, you may want to have the student complete the Skills Review or the *Voyager 2* Skills Preview to determine if that book is more appropriate.

Working through the Lessons

The individual lesson notes on pages 43–62 provide teaching suggestions for each lesson.

Working with the Reading Selections

The reading selection is the heart of each lesson. To help students better understand the reading, read the title aloud. Ask students to look at the picture. Ask them what they think the reading will be about.

The following suggestions depend on class size:

▶ **One-on-one tutoring:** Skim the selection to determine whether the student will be able to read it independently or will need assistance.

- If you think the student can read the selection independently, have him or her read it aloud to you. If the student mispronounces or skips a word, let him or her continue to read, see that the sentence did not make sense, and correct the error. If the student does not self-correct after one or two sentences, wait until he or she has finished reading and have the student reread the incorrect sentence.
- If you think the student will need assistance, try one of the assisted reading strategies described on page 10 in this guide.

▶ **Group instruction:** Skim the selection and use one of these strategies, depending on the difficulty of the selection:

- If you think students will need assistance, try one of the assisted reading strategies described on page 10 in this guide.
- Read the entire selection aloud to students. Then have students read it to themselves. Next, have individual students each read a sentence or paragraph aloud.

- Read the first paragraph aloud to students. Then have volunteers read the remaining paragraphs aloud. Finally, have students read the entire selection to themselves.

Using the Answer Key (p. 120)

Check students' answers as they complete an exercise or lesson. You may consider letting advanced students check and correct their own work.

Using the Reference Handbook (p. 125)

Here are some tips:
- Selected Words in *Voyager 1* (does not include most one-syllable short-vowel words) Students can use the list to practice looking up words arranged alphabetically. They can also check the spelling of written answers. Instructors can use the list to create extension activities—flash cards, sentence building, categories, etc.
- Writing Skills Rules (a summary of the spelling and mechanics rules in the mini-lessons) Have students refer to this page whenever they are doing the editing step of Write About It in the unit reviews.

Using the Skills Review (p. 115)

Have students complete the review independently. Use the Skills Review Answers and Evaluation Chart to evaluate students' performance. Read students' Write About It pieces and give them feedback on all parts of the writing process.

Discuss the review results with students. If a student struggled through or performed poorly on a section of the Skills Review, assess the problem area(s). You may want the student to review the lessons and/or units in which these areas are covered.

Finally, have students return to the Student Interest Inventory (*Voyager 1*, page 6) and fill out the right side of the chart. Discuss their progress and ongoing goals.

Voyager 1 Teacher's Notes

Pre-Assessment

Before you begin Unit 1 with students, be sure they have completed the Student Interest Inventory and the Skills Preview at the beginning of *Voyager 1* (see pages 6 and 8).

In addition to *Voyager 1*, students will need
- a folder in which to keep their work-in-progress and finished work (see page 12)
- a spiral-bound or three-ring notebook to use as a personal dictionary (see page 9)
- a spiral-bound or three-ring notebook to use as a personal spelling list (see page 12)

▶ Unit 1: Hopes and Dreams

Part of Unit	*Voyager 1* pages	TRG pages	Workbook pages
Overview	11	43	
Lesson 1	12 – 19	43 – 45	4 – 5
Lesson 2	20 – 27	45 – 46	6 – 7
Lesson 3	28 – 33	46 – 47	8 – 9
Writing Skills Mini-Lesson	34	47	10 – 11
Unit 1 Review	35 – 36	47	12 – 13

Student Objectives

Reading
- Read two stories and a poem.
- Practice the strategies of using prior experience, background knowledge, and visualizing.
- Understand sequence, cause and effect, and the main idea.

Writing
- Make a list; write two poems.
- Learn about sentences and capitalization.

Phonics
- Review the short vowels.
- Practice five initial blends: *br, cl, gr, pl, st.*
- Practice five final blends: *ft, ld, mp, nt, st.*

▶ Unit 1 Photocopy Masters (PCMs)
PCM 11: Cause-and-Effect Chart
PCM 12: Sequence Time Line
PCM 13: Word Work (Units 1 and 2)
PCM 15: Student Progress Tracking Sheet
PCM 18: Phonics Elements in *Foundation Book* and *Voyager 1*

▶ Personal Dictionaries and Spelling Lists
Encourage students to choose words they would like to learn to add to their dictionaries and spelling lists during each lesson (see pages 9 and 12).

Unit 1 Overview (p. 11)

The Unit Overview introduces the theme "Hopes and Dreams." Discuss the picture. Ask, *"What can you guess about these people's hopes and dreams?"* Record students' responses on the board. Read the overview aloud. Then do a paired reading with students (see "Increasing Fluency," page 10). Discuss students' answers to the questions in the last paragraph.

Lesson 1 (pp. 12–19)

Learning Goals Discuss the learning goals.

Before You Read Read the introduction to the story aloud. Explain that students can use their life experiences to help them understand what they read, and that they will use this strategy in Lesson 1.

1. Read the questions aloud. List students' reasons for wanting to read better.
2. Have students check off their reasons and copy two others from those listed on the board.

Key Words The underlined words are important to the meaning of the reading. Have students try to use context to figure out each key word. Then write the key words on the board. Ask students to read them aloud and to write any words they want to learn in their personal dictionaries.

As You Read Read the text aloud. Remind students to think about their own decision to improve their reading skills.

"A Class of Hopes" Follow one of the reading strategies on page 10. After each paragraph is read, ask students to pick out the picture that matches the character. This will help them see the relationship between the story and the pictures.

After You Read Read each question aloud and discuss with students. For questions 1 and 2, ask, *"How do you know that?"* Write responses to question 3 on the board.

▶ *Special notes:* Point out that each character's name starts with a capital letter. Have students circle all the names. Ask them what other words in the story start with capital letters. Have students underline the first word in each sentence. Explain that sentences begin with a capital letter.

▶ **Extending the reading:** Ask students to interview each other for five minutes, asking *"If you learn to read better, how will your life be different in five years?"* Have students report on their interviews.

Think About It: Sequencing Events

1. Read the definition of *sequence* aloud. Introduce the concept using an everyday example, such as getting ready for bed. Write *First, Then, Last* on the board. Have students find and underline these sequence words on page 14.
2. Explain that many stories are organized by sequence, or the order in which events occur.

3. Read the alarm clock sequence aloud. Encourage students to describe their own morning routines using *first, then,* and *last.*

Practice: Read the directions. Have students complete the activities either as a group, in pairs, or individually. Then have them discuss their answers.

▶ **Extending the skill**

1. Ask, *"What else besides stories can be written in a sequence?"* (directions). Ask students to dictate or write directions for getting to another room in your class's building using the words *first, then,* and *last.*
2. Use PCM 12 to introduce a sequence with the four sequence words *first, second, then,* and *last.* Ask students to dictate or write directions on how to do something in four steps.
3. Using a minimal-text cartoon strip, cut apart the frames and mix them up. Let pairs of students sequence them and read them aloud.

Write About It: Make a List Explain that making lists is an important writing skill used in daily life. Ask if students make lists and, if so, what kinds.

A. Discuss "Brad's Plan" with students. Point out that apostrophes show possession (*Brad's*). Make sure that students know that *GED* stands for *General Educational Development.*

B. Have students recopy "Brad's Plan" on the lines.

C. Students will generate their own writing ideas. Encourage independent work, but answer any questions they have. Take dictation if needed. Review students' drafts (**C2**) before they recopy them (see pages 11–12, "Working with Adult New Writers," for more ideas).

Word Work: Short Vowels (*a, e, i, o, u*)

A. Read the names of the vowels aloud; have students repeat.

1. Say the short *a* sound. Have students repeat.
2. Read the list of short *a* words. Have students repeat each word after you read it.
3. Have students say the short *a* word list.
4. Repeat this process for the other word lists.

B. Model the exercise using *pet* and *pot.* Have students complete the exercise.

C. Read the directions. Using the first column as an example, demonstrate how to try out vowels to decide which ones make real words. Have students complete the exercise in small groups.

D. Read the definition and discuss word families. Stress that words in a word family contain letters in common and that the words rhyme (see "Working with Word Families," page 29). Read the first word in the first list. Ask students to read the rest and to add a word to the family. Do the same with the other word families.

▶ **Extending the skill:** Have students cut apart appropriate letters and word families from PCM 13. Show them how to combine letters and word families to form words. Have them work in pairs to form as many words as possible. Have them say each new word aloud. Students should keep their letters for future use.

Update Read or have students read this aloud. Discuss students' ideas about the question.

▶ **More Practice:** *Voyager 1 Workbook* p. 4

Help students fill out copies of PCM 15 to include in their working folders.

Lesson 2 (pp. 20–27)

Learning Goals Discuss the learning goals.

Before You Read Read the introduction. Explain that what they already know about moving to a new place can help students understand the reading.

Read part 1 aloud. Students can write about themselves or others. Write students' dictated answers; let them copy. Read the directions to part 2 aloud. Have students read the reasons and check the ones they agree with. Write other reasons students give on the board and let them copy one.

Key Words See Lesson 1 notes. Point out that names of people, countries, and languages are capitalized.

▶ **Extension:** Let students dictate and copy sentences using the key words.

As You Read Read the text aloud. Remind students to relate what they are reading to what they know.

"A New Life" Before reading, discuss the picture. Ask, *"What dreams does Sal have?"* Follow one of the reading strategies on page 10.

After You Read Have students retell the story in a chain, with each student completing one of the sentence starters. Give them the option of adding a sentence of their own. Record students' answers.

▶ **Extending the reading:** Discuss the hardships Sal may have faced and how he may have overcome them. You might say, *"Imagine finding yourself in a strange country one day. How would you feel? What would you do?"*

Think About It: Identifying Cause and Effect Read the definitions aloud and discuss the meaning of cause and effect. Discuss the pictures. Ask for and record other examples (a lighted match causing a fire; a big meal causing drowsiness).

Practice: Read the directions for **A** and **B.** Have students discuss the pictures. Have students read their sentences in part **C** aloud.

▶ **Extending the skill:** Ask students to think about cause-and-effect situations in their everyday lives (e.g., the effect of forgetting to put money in a parking meter). Pass out copies of PCM 11 and ask students to write one cause and the effect on the PCM. Then have students describe the effect and let the others guess the cause.

Write About It: Write a Poem Read the poem aloud. Then do a paired reading with students (see page 10). "Sal's Poem" serves as a model for what the students will do. It is an example of free verse, having an irregular metrical pattern and lines that do not rhyme. Discuss the form of the poem: first and last name on the first and last lines; descriptive words about Sal on line 2; names of Sal's relatives on lines 3 and 4; details about Sal on lines 5–8.

A. Read the directions. Ask students to compare the sentence starters to Sal's poem. Then have students dictate or write a draft of their own poem. Have them read it aloud.

B–C. Introduce the writing process by discussing drafts. Explain that when we revise, we add, cut, or replace material to improve a draft. Let students revise, using the steps in **B.** Don't focus on spelling, punctuation, or other mechanics at this point, unless students ask specific questions. Have students copy their final drafts in **C,** and then read them aloud. They might also illustrate their poems or add a photo (see "Working with Adult New Writers" on pages 11–12 for more ideas).

Word Work: Initial Consonant Blends (*br, cl, gr, pl, st*) Explain that blends contain two or more consonants. When we say a blend, we hear the sound for each letter, but the sounds are close together. Write the blend *br* on the board. Write the word *brave* under it. Say the word, then have students repeat it. Be sure they can hear both sounds in the *br* blend. Discourage students from adding a vowel sound to the blend (e.g., *buh-ruh*). The added sound will make it harder to decode words effectively.

A. Read the directions. Have students underline the consonant blend *br-* in all the words in column 1. Have them say the words they know. Tell them the other words and have students repeat them. Ask volunteers to use each word in a sentence. Repeat this process for each list.

B. Read the directions and model the exercise using *clock* and *crock*. Have students complete the exercise.

▶ **Extending the skill:** In random order, read the words not pictured and have students find them.

C. Review the definition of word families. Follow the process in Lesson 1 notes.

D. Read the directions. Use example 1 to demonstrate how to fill in the blank. Say, *"'Blank' came to the U.S. from Mexico."* Ask, *"Does* Pal or Sal *fit the sentence better?"* Let students complete the exercise individually or in pairs.

▶ **Extending the skill:** Have students cut apart appropriate letters and word families from PCM 13 and add them to the ones from Lesson 1 to form new words.

Update Read or have students read this aloud. Discuss what Sal's brother might do when he comes to the U.S.

▶ **More Practice:** *Voyager 1 Workbook* p. 6

Help students fill out copies of PCM 15.

Lesson 3 (pp. 28–33)

Learning Goals Discuss the learning goals. Discuss the strategy of visualizing; explain that by mentally picturing what they read, students will better understand "Dreams."

Before You Read Read the introduction. Explain that poets choose specific words to convey images (mental pictures) and emotions. Point out that readers should try to picture the images as they read.

Read, record, and discuss student responses to questions 1–3. Let students copy or try to write their own answers.

Discuss the picture on page 29. Ask what feelings or ideas about dreams the picture brings to mind.

Key Words See Lesson 1 notes.

As You Read Read the text aloud. Remind students to visualize as they read the poem.

"Dreams" Read the poem to students. Then conduct a paired or echo reading (see page 10). Finally, have students read the poem aloud.

After You Read Read and discuss each question. Discuss how the images in the poem convey meaning and emotions. Ask if the picture on page 29 helped students understand the poem better.

▶ **Extending the reading:** Discuss the format of poems—they're often short; they usually have a marked rhythm; they often rhyme. Many poems use repetition. Discuss how "Dreams" differs in form from the poem students wrote in Lesson 2. Ask what other poems students have seen.

Encourage students to practice reading "Dreams" aloud. Have volunteers read it at your next session.

Think About It: Understanding the Main Idea Discuss the definition of main idea. Reread the poem and ask students what they think the main idea is. Let students read the first line of "Dreams" aloud. Ask them if they agree that the main idea is "Hold on to your dreams." Read the second paragraph and have students read the rest of the first stanza. Discuss this image of a life without dreams.

Practice Discuss each question. Write possible answers on the board. Have students copy the answers they like best. Have them discuss their answers to the last question in pairs or small groups.

▶ **Extending the skill:** Have students reread "A Class of Hopes" on *Voyager 1*, page 13, and pick the sentence that describes the main idea of the story. ("Ken, Jan, and Brad all hope for better lives.")

Write About It: Write a Poem Read the introduction. Then have students read both poems aloud. Discuss the similarities in form and content and have students point out the differences. Ask about the images that the new poem brings to mind.

A–B. Read the directions aloud. Discuss how the title indicates the main idea of the poem. Have students underline words that they would like to change in "Let Go." Let them write the changes on the lines in part **B.** Have students read their poems and make revisions. Let students copy their new poems on separate paper and put the copies in their working folders.

Word Work: Final Consonant Blends (*ft, ld, mp, nt, st***)** Review the concept of blends. Point out that blends can be found at the beginning or end of words. Give some examples.

A–C. Follow the process described in Lesson 2.
D. Crossword Puzzle Have students read the words they know aloud. Teach the other words. Fit *own* and *winged* into the puzzle. Have students complete the puzzle in pairs.

▶ **Extending the skill:** Have students cut apart appropriate letters and word families from PCM 13 and form new words.

▶ **More Practice:** *Voyager 1 Workbook* p. 8

Help students fill out copies of PCM 15.

Writing Skills Mini-Lesson: Sentences and Capitalization (p. 34)

1. Read the introduction aloud. Read rule 1 and the example aloud and discuss. Write other examples on the board. Make sure students understand what a complete thought is. You may want to write one or two fragments and ask students to explain why each is not a sentence.
2. Read rule 2 and discuss it. Ask students to supply other examples. Write them on the board.
3. Read rule 3 and discuss it. Ask which example is a question.

Practice: Read the directions aloud to make sure students understand what to do. Have students work in pairs, compare answers, and give each other feedback. Review students' work.

▶ **More Practice:** *Voyager 1 Workbook* p. 10

Unit 1 Review (pp. 35–36)

Explain that this review will help students evaluate what they have learned in Unit 1. If necessary, read aloud or have volunteers read the story before students begin to answer the questions. Make sure students know how to do each part of the review. Have them complete the Reading Review and the Word Work Review as independently as possible.

Introduce the writing process in Write About It. Read the topic aloud. Go over the five steps of the Writing Process. You may want students to complete this activity in class the first time. When they get to the editing step, point out that they should check for complete sentences, correct capitalization, and correct punctuation (see pages 11–12, "Working with Adult New Writers," for more ideas).

▶ **More Practice:** *Voyager 1 Workbook* p. 12

▶ *Final note:* Review with students the copies of PCM 15 that they have placed in their working folders. Ask what additional help they think they need with material from the three lessons and the writing skills mini-lesson in Unit 1. Discuss possible ways of meeting their needs.

▶ Unit 2: Everyday Heroes

Part of Unit	*Voyager 1* pages	TRG pages	Workbook pages
Overview	37	48	
Lesson 4	38 – 45	48 – 49	14 – 15
Lesson 5	46 – 53	50 – 51	16 – 17
Lesson 6	54 – 59	51 – 52	18 – 19
Writing Skills Mini-Lesson	60	52	20 – 21
Unit 2 Review	61 – 62	52	22 – 23

Student Objectives

Reading

- Read about two real people; read a news article and a poem.
- Use the reading strategies of background knowledge, visualizing, and prior experience.
- Predict, find details, and make inferences.

Writing

- Write about a reading; interview and write about a person; write a paragraph.
- Learn about contractions using *not*.

Phonics

- Learn the long vowel sounds: *a, e, i, o, u,* and *y*.

▶ Unit 2 Photocopy Masters (PCMs)

PCM 9: Five W's Chart
PCM 10: Detail Diagram
PCM 13: Word Work (Units 1 and 2)
PCM 15: Student Progress Tracking Sheet
PCM 18: Phonics Elements in *Foundation Book* and *Voyager 1*

▶ Personal Dictionaries and Spelling Lists

Encourage students to add words to their dictionaries and spelling lists during each lesson in Unit 2.

Unit 2 Overview (p. 37)

The overview introduces the "Everyday Heroes" theme with a collage of pictures. The heroes pictured include Rosa Parks, Cesar Chavez, and fictional characters. Discuss the pictures. Ask, *"Have you heard of Rosa Parks or Cesar Chavez? What did they do to be thought of as heroes?"* Read the overview aloud, then do a paired reading. Discuss the questions in the last paragraph.

Lesson 4 (pp. 38–45)

Learning Goals Discuss the learning goals.

Before You Read Explain that making predictions before and during reading helps a reader anticipate what to expect next. When they compare their predictions to what actually occurs, students become more active readers. Students will practice this skill in Lesson 4. They will also use their prior knowledge to better understand "A Bus Ride."

Read the introduction and question 1 aloud. Write volunteers' predictions on the board and have students copy them on the blank lines. Discuss questions 2 and 3. Be prepared to provide details about the civil rights movement.

Key Words See Lesson 1 notes. Point out the prefix *un-* in *unfair.* Explain that it means *not.* Have students list and define other words that begin with *un-.* If you would like, let students dictate and copy their own sentences using the key words.

As You Read Tell students to remember what they know about the civil rights movement as they read.

"A Bus Ride" Follow one of the reading strategies on page 10.

After You Read
A. Read the directions. Have students use the sentence starters to retell "A Bus Ride" in their own words. Record responses. Then have students copy the responses on their own paper. Have them read their versions aloud.

B. Ask students why they think Rosa Parks is considered a hero.

▶ **Extending the reading:** Discuss the differences between nonfiction (factual writing) and fiction (made-up stories). Have students tell why "A Bus Ride" is nonfiction. (Rosa Parks is a real person. The event really happened.) Have students name and discuss other examples of nonfiction (biographies, news articles, historical accounts).

Think About It: Making Predictions Ask students how making predictions helps them every day (weather forecasting, estimating grocery costs, etc.). Then discuss why making predictions can help reading comprehension. Tell students that by predicting and checking those predictions, readers are continually interacting with the reading. This "active reading" approach helps readers pay attention to and better understand what they read.

Read the introduction. Discuss the types of clues available for predicting reading content. Discuss students' earlier predictions about "A Bus Ride."

Practice: Read the directions. Have students do parts **A–C;** review their answers. For **B** and **C,** students can work in pairs. Point out that different predictions can be valid. (Jan will like this job, *or* Jan will sell the dress.)

▶ **Extending the skill:** Bring in and/or have students bring in books that have jackets or covers with pictures, such as romances, westerns, and biographies. Based on the covers, have students predict what each book will be about. Discuss their predictions and their reasons for making them.

Write About It: Write About What You Read
Explain that writing about a story helps us to see how well we remember and understand it.

A–B. Read "A Hero to Farm Workers" with students and discuss it. Discuss the predictions students made in part **C** on page 41. Record any additional facts that students know about Chavez, the UFW, or unions in general.

C. Have students retell the story by completing the sentence starters. Have volunteers read

their writing aloud (see pages 11–12, "Working with Adult New Writers," for more ideas).

Word Work: Long *a* and Long *i*
a-e, ai,* and *ay* = Long *a
A. Read the introduction. Point out the three common ways the long *a* sound can be spelled.
- Say the sound for long *a.* Have students repeat it.
- Read the long *a* words in the first column aloud. Ask students to listen for the sound. Have students read each long *a* word aloud.
- Repeat this process for *ai* and *ay.*

B. Read the directions. Read *ran* and *rain* aloud and make sure students can hear the difference between the short and long *a* sounds. Have students complete the exercise.

C. Read the directions and the example. Have students do the exercise, giving help if necessary.

D. Discuss the patterns that students discern.

i-e* and *igh* = Long *i
E–G. Repeat process used for **A, C,** and **D.**

H. Read the directions. Be sure students recognize the two pronunciations for *live.*

I. Follow the process in Lesson 1 notes.

J. Read the words in the box. Demonstrate how to do fill-in-the-blank exercises by saying, *"Rosa Parks took a bus 'blank.' What word in the box completes the sentence?"* Demonstrate the process of elimination by reading the sentence with *admire, life,* and *ride* in the blank. When students identify *ride* as the correct answer, tell them to check off the word in the box and write it on the line. Let students complete the activity individually or in pairs. Then have students read their sentences aloud.

▶ **Extending the skill:** Have students cut apart appropriate letters and word families from PCM 13 and form new words.

Update Read or have students read this aloud. Discuss other civil rights leaders students know of.

▶ **More Practice:** *Voyager 1 Workbook* p. 14

Help students fill out copies of PCM 15.

Lesson 5 (pp. 46–53)

Learning Goals Discuss the learning goals.

Before You Read Tell students that they will use the strategy of visualizing—picturing what they read—to better understand the reading in this lesson. Read, discuss, and record student responses to questions 1–3. Let them copy their answers to 2 and 3 on the lines provided.

Key Words See Lesson 1 notes. If students ask about the silent *k* in *known,* explain that *k* is silent when followed by *n.* Give a few other examples (*knife, knee, knot*).

As You Read Read the strategy reminder aloud.

"Neighbor Saves Family" Explain that this reading is a news article. Discuss the picture and headline. Follow one of the reading strategies on page 10. Encourage students to picture Steve's actions as they read.

After You Read Read the directions aloud; discuss the questions. Then discuss each feature of the article: the headline, photo, caption, factual information, quotations, etc.

▶ **Extending the reading:** Have the class create a brief news article about a recent local event. Be sure their article contains the features listed above. They can be creative with the photo and the quotations, but the facts should be as accurate as possible. Write the article on the board; revise and edit it as a class. Have students copy the edited version and put it in their working folders.

Think About It: Finding Details Discuss the definition of *details.* Explain that details support main ideas and provide relevant information.

A. Read the directions and the first sentence. Demonstrate how to check **True** or **False.** After students complete the exercise, review it together. Then have students correct the false statements to make them true.

B. Read the directions and model how to look back at the story to complete sentence 1. Have students complete the exercise in pairs. Discuss their answers.

Practice: Discuss the picture and headline. Make sure students recognize the fire fighter from the article on page 47. Read this article aloud. Then have students echo-read it. Working in pairs, have students find details to complete the sentences.

▶ **Extending the skill:** Use PCM 10 to show how details relate to the main idea. Have students work in pairs to write "Pete Greeley Retires" in the main idea oval. Then have them copy details from the news article into the detail boxes.

Write About It: Write About a Person You Interview Explain that reporters get information by asking questions. Read the introduction aloud and have students read the "Five W" words in the box. Discuss the Five W's and their special value in gathering details.

A. Read the directions. Go over the example and remind students to check off answers as they use them. Let students work independently to complete the exercise. Have them review their work together.

B. Read the introduction and review the five W's. Read the questions aloud, saying *blank* when needed. Have students complete all six questions, giving help as needed. Let students practice asking the questions. Then pair students for interviews and have them write their partner's answers on the lines.

C. Do 1 as an example to show students how to turn the questions and responses in part **B** into statements in part **C.** Have them complete the exercise and read their interview results aloud (see pages 11–12, "Working with Adult New Writers" for more ideas).

▶ **Extending the skill:** Find or adapt a simple news article and give each student a copy. Have students use PCM 9 to write details found in the article. If needed, ask the "Five W's" (e.g., *"Who is this about?" "Where did it happen?"*).

Word Work: Long *e* and Long *y*

e, ee* and *e-e* = Long *e

A. Follow the process used for long *a* in Lesson 4.
B. Read the directions aloud. Make sure students understand that *ea* can make three different

sounds. Read the words in each column and have students repeat them.

C. Explain that *ea* in *read* can be a long or short *e*. Tell students that the pronunciation is determined by the meaning of the sentence.

y as a Long Vowel

D. Follow the process for long *a* in Lesson 4.

Practice

E. Read the words in the box aloud. Have students complete the sentences and read them aloud.

F. Read the directions and go over the example with students. Emphasize that they are to cross out words that don't have long vowel sounds. Go over students' answers with them.

▶ **Extending the skill:** Have students cut apart appropriate letters and word families from PCM 13 and form new words.

Update Read or have students read this aloud. Discuss the value of smoke detectors and the purposes of Neighborhood Watch groups.

▶ **More Practice:** *Voyager 1 Workbook* p. 16

Help students fill out copies of PCM 15.

Lesson 6 (pp. 54–59)

Learning Goals Discuss the learning goals.

Before You Read Explain that students will use their life experiences to help them understand the poem in Lesson 6. Tell students they can use this strategy to better understand almost anything they read. Read and discuss the introduction and questions 1–3. Record the responses and have students copy them on the lines provided. Students can make up a situation for questions 1 and 2, if they wish.

Key Words See Lesson 1 notes. Point out the contractions and explain that two words have been combined and some letters left out. Discuss what words *couldn't* and *can't* were formed from. Explain that students will learn more about contractions at the end of this unit.

As You Read Read the text and discuss the picture. Remind students to use what they know about poems to help them understand this one.

"Can't" Read the poem aloud, then conduct a paired or echo reading.

After You Read

A. Have each student read the poem aloud.

B. Read each question aloud and discuss. You can record student answers to question 4. You may want to tally how many students respond "yourself" and how many say "other people."

▶ **Extending the reading:** In pairs, let students act out the poem using the roles of narrator and challenger. Encourage them to be demonstrative.

Think About It: Making Inferences Read the definition aloud. Discuss how we make inferences by looking at clues or other information to figure something out or draw a conclusion (infer). Clothing can provide good examples of how we make inferences about seasons (e.g., a bathing suit suggests summer while snow boots imply winter).

Look at the picture clues. Have students read the inferences and discuss what clues make the inferences correct. Ask, *"Can you infer anything else about these pictures?"* (the woman was prepared for rain; the man has a dog; the man is a good carpenter). Record students' reasonable inferences; let them copy them onto the lesson page.

Practice: Read the directions aloud. Have students read the words in the box. Let students complete the riddles. Have volunteers read them aloud.

▶ **Extending the skill:** Bring in at least 10 picture-based magazine or newspaper ads. Discuss the purpose of ads—to convince consumers to buy certain products. Explain that ads often imply things rather than saying them outright. For instance, an ad may imply that wearing a given brand of perfume will make you glamorous or that buying a certain kind of car will make you seem younger.

Have students work in small groups. Give each group several ads and ask them to infer the message of each ad. Encourage them to ask questions, such as *"Why is this product better than another?"* *"How will a consumer feel when he or she owns this product?"* *"What makes this product special?"* Have the groups write their inferences and present them, along with the ads, to the class. Have them explain what led them to each inference.

Write About It: Write a Paragraph Read the introduction and directions aloud. It may be helpful if you discuss something that was hard for you to try, so that students feel comfortable with this exercise.

A. Read the sentence starters aloud. Then let students complete them independently. If students can't think of a personal experience to write about, suggest that they write about someone else or imagine an experience.

B. Before students write a paragraph, have them read their sentences to a partner for comments. Help students with spelling if they ask. Point out that a paragraph does not begin a new sentence on each line (see pages 11–12, "Working with Adult New Writers," for more ideas).

Word Work: Long *o* and Long *u*

A. Follow the process for long *a* in Lesson 4.

B. Demonstrate the two sounds for *u: yoo* as in *use* and *oo* as in *June*. Make sure students can hear and say both sounds. Follow the process used for long *a* in Lesson 4. Point out that the way a word is spelled does not indicate the way the *u* is pronounced.

C. Read the directions aloud. Remind students how to read and listen for the long vowel sounds. Let students complete the exercise. As a check, have students read aloud the words remaining in each line.

D. Follow the process in Lesson 1 notes.

E. Read the directions and the word pairs in the box aloud. Use the example to demonstrate how to do the exercise. Point out that the underlined "clue" lets students know which word family to use.

F. Have students work in pairs or small groups to write rhymes. Tell them the rhymes can be funny or nonsensical.

▶ **Extending the skill:** Have students cut apart appropriate letters and word families from PCM 13 and form new words.

▶ **More Practice:** *Voyager 1 Workbook* p. 18

Help students fill out copies of PCM 15.

Writing Skills Mini-Lesson: Contractions (p. 60)

This mini-lesson focuses on contractions with *not*. Read the definition aloud. Demonstrate how to write an apostrophe. Explain that it tells the reader where one or more letters have been omitted. Read each pair of words aloud; ask students to read the corresponding contraction. Then have students work in pairs to read the words and contractions.

Practice

A. Let students find and copy the correct contractions.

B. Read the directions aloud; check students' work on question 1 before they do 2 and 3.

▶ **More Practice:** *Voyager 1 Workbook* p. 20

Unit 2 Review (pp. 61–62)

Follow the process described in Unit 1.

As students work through the writing process, point out that when they edit their writing, they should check that contractions with *not* are spelled correctly.

▶ **Extending the skill:** Have students use all the letters and word families from PCM 13 to practice forming words. You may make a game of it, timing students to see how many words they can create in five minutes. Have students keep their letters in an envelope for future use.

▶ **More Practice:** *Voyager 1 Workbook* p. 22

▶ *Final note:* Review with students the copies of PCM 15 that they have placed in their working folders. Ask what additional help they think they need with material from the three lessons and the writing skills mini-lesson in Unit 2. Discuss possible ways of meeting their needs.

► Unit 3: Thrilling Moments

Part of Unit	*Voyager 1* pages	TRG pages	Workbook pages
Overview	63	53	
Lesson 7	64–71	53–54	24–25
Lesson 8	72–79	54–56	26–27
Lesson 9	80–85	56–57	28–29
Writing Skills Mini-Lesson	86	57	30–31
Unit 3 Review	87–88	57	32–33

Student Objectives

Reading
- Read two stories and a poem.
- Use the reading strategies of prior experience, background knowledge, and visualizing.
- Identify cause and effect; understand sequence; make inferences.

Writing
- Write a story and a poem; make a list.
- Learn how to form plural words.

Phonics
- Learn five digraphs: *sh, ch, th, ph, wh.*
- Learn five 3-letter initial blends: *scr, spl, spr, str, thr.*
- Learn five 3-letter final blends: *nch, nce, nge, rse, dge.*

► Unit 3 PCMs
PCM 9: Five W's Chart
PCM 10: Detail Diagram
PCM 11: Cause-and-Effect Chart
PCM 12: Sequence Time Line
PCM 13: Word Work (Units 1 and 2)
PCM 14: Word Work (Units 3 and 4)
PCM 15: Student Progress Tracking Sheet
PCM 18: Phonics Elements in *Foundation Book* and *Voyager 1*

► Personal Dictionaries and Spelling Lists
Encourage students to add words to their dictionaries and spelling lists during each lesson.

Unit 3 Overview (p. 63)

Discuss the picture. Ask, *"What do you think the people were thrilled about?"* Read the overview aloud; follow with a paired reading. Discuss the questions in the last paragraph.

Lesson 7 (pp. 64–71)

Learning Goals Discuss the learning goals.

Before You Read Read the introduction aloud. Tell students that they will use the strategy of prior experience to better understand "The Promotion."
1. Read the questions aloud. Discuss and record students' examples of thrilling moments.
2. Have students check off the sentences that are true for them and write two other examples on the lines. If students can't think of personal experiences, suggest that they list something someone else has done.

Key Words See Lesson 1 notes. Ask students why *Ms. Chin* is capitalized. Point out that *Alpha Company* (name of a company) and *Thursday* (day of the week) are also capitalized.

As You Read Read the text aloud. Remind students to think about their own experiences to help them understand the reading.

"The Promotion" Read the title; discuss the picture. Ask, *"What can you tell about the people in the picture?"* Follow one of the reading strategies on page 10.

After You Read Read each question aloud and discuss the causes and effects in the story.

► **Extending the reading:** Have students work in teams to describe or invent a problem at school or work. Let them write the problem down and trade problems with other teams. Each team then brainstorms solutions for five minutes.

Think About It: Identifying Cause and Effect Review the concept of cause and effect by reading the introduction aloud. Have students explain the cause and the effect in the example.

Practice

A. Read the directions aloud. Remind students to check off each effect as they match it to a cause. Have volunteers explain their answers.

B. Read the directions. Have students read the sentences silently and choose the effect for each cause. Let students review their answers in pairs—one student reading the cause and the partner reading the effect.

C. Read the directions and the answer list aloud. Alternatively, let students read the list silently. Have students read the first cause, choose the correct effect, and copy it on the line. Let them finish the exercise in class or as homework.

Write About It: Write a Story

Read the introduction. Explain that a proverb is a short saying that expresses an obvious truth or familiar experience. Give an example. Ask volunteers to say proverbs that they know.

A. Read or have students read the first part of each proverb. Have them match proverb endings and read the proverbs aloud.

B. Have students work in pairs to read and discuss the proverbs and rephrase them. Point out that the "if . . . then" construction shows cause and effect in plainer language.

C–D. Read the directions. Have students complete the proverbs and read them aloud. If no one can think of an ending, write one on the board for them. Help students to find other proverbs for **D** if necessary.

E. Let students write as independently as possible. Have them read their stories aloud (see pages 11–12, "Working with Adult New Writers," for more ideas).

▶ **Extending the skill:** Have students use PCM 11 to organize one or more ideas for a story. Have them describe a cause-and-effect experience and write a short story describing it.

Word Work: Digraphs (*ch, sh, th, ph, wh*)

A. Read the introduction. Explain that a digraph is a pair of letters that spell a single sound.
   1. Say the *ch* sound. Have students repeat it.
   2. Read the *ch* words aloud and ask students to listen for the sound. Have students read each *ch* word aloud.
   3. Repeat this process for each digraph list. Explain that there are two sounds for *th*. Say *thin* and *than*. Can students hear the difference? Ask students to repeat the words. Can they make the two sounds?

B–C. Read the directions. Do the first one of each exercise with students. Let them complete the exercises independently or in pairs.

D. Read the directions. Using the *shone* example, show students how to match a digraph to a word family to make a word. Point out that the second word-family word they write does not have to begin with a digraph. Help students complete the exercise if necessary.

E. Read the directions. When students have completed the exercise, have them read all of the sentences aloud as a story.

▶ **Extending the skill:** Have students cut apart appropriate letter groups from PCM 14 and use them with letters and word families from PCM 13 to form new words.

Update Have students read this aloud. Discuss the pros and cons of changing jobs, departments, or even companies.

▶ **More Practice:** *Voyager 1 Workbook* p. 24

Help students fill out copies of PCM 15.

Lesson 8 (pp. 72–79)

Learning Goals Discuss the learning goals.

Before You Read Explain that students will use their background knowledge about marathons to better understand "The Thrill of the Race." Have students read and discuss questions 1–3. Elicit as much information about marathons as possible. Be prepared to provide background information.

Key Words See Lesson 1 notes. Point out the capital letters in *Boston Marathon* and *Patriots' Day*.

As You Read Read the strategy reminder and discuss the picture.

"The Thrill of the Race" Follow one of the reading strategies on page 10.

After You Read

A. Ask students to close their books. Remind them that retelling a story helps to show how well they understood it. Start the retelling with *"Phyllis Jones likes to run."* Let each student add a sentence. Write down all the sentences. Then compare the students' story with the original. If their version is much changed from the original, students may need more work on reading comprehension. You could reread the story to students, having them close their eyes and visualize what is happening. Then they can repeat the retelling process (see page 10, "Improving Comprehension," for more ideas).

B. Read the directions aloud and discuss.

▶ **Extending the reading:** Have students use PCM 9 and PCM 10 to find details about the Boston Marathon in "The Thrill of the Race." Have them answer the Five W's. Point out that there can be more than one answer for each question. For example, "Who?" can be Phyllis Jones, her friends, or 5,000 runners. Students should list as many details on the chart as they can find.

Think About It: Sequencing Events Review the definition of *sequence*. Have students look at the clocks and read the sentences silently. Point out that the first word in each sentence is a sequence word that tells when something happened. Write *First, Second, Then,* and *Last* on the board. Point out that *second* is a new sequence word.

Practice

A. Read the directions. Let students read the words in the box aloud. Read aloud and discuss the sentences and their correct order, pointing out that the first sentence in the sequence is already numbered *1*. Have students number and write the correct sequence word for each sentence. Have them read the sentences aloud in the correct sequence.

B. Read the introduction. Have students work in pairs or small groups to discuss the pictures (which are in sequence). Let them use the pictures to number and complete the sentences.

C. Have students copy the four sentences in order in paragraph format and write a title. Students can practice reading aloud by reading their paragraphs to partners.

▶ **Extending the skill:** Hand out copies of PCM 12. Using the example on the PCM, show how time lines show sequence from left to right. Have students fill out a time line with a sequence of events from their own lives.

Write About It: Make a List Read the introduction.

A. Use the first line to show how to unscramble the sentences of the invitation. If students have trouble, have them copy each word onto a piece of paper and then put the words in order.

B. Read the directions. Have students read the sentences, discuss their proper order, and copy them on the right lines. Have students read their completed sentences aloud.

C–D. Read the directions. Have the class brainstorm other tasks that need to be done for a party. Write their ideas on the board. Have students choose tasks to copy into their books. Let them number their lists in order and copy them onto the lines in part **D** (see pages 11–12, "Working with Adult New Writers," for more ideas).

Word Work: Three-letter Initial Blends (*scr, spl, spr, str, thr*) Remind students that when they say a consonant blend, they hear the sound for each letter, but the sounds are close together. Point out that students will hear three sounds in the *s* blends. Write the first blend, *scr*, on the board. Write the word *scrap* under it. Say the word; then have students repeat it. Be sure they can hear the three sounds. Repeat with the other blends. When you come to *thr*, note that, since *th* is a digraph, only two sounds are heard.

A. Read the directions. Have students underline the consonant blend *scr* in all the words in column 1. Let them say the words they know. Tell them the other words and have students repeat them. Have students read the word list. Let volunteers use each word in a sentence. Repeat this process for each list.

Be sure students can tell the difference between a three- and a two-letter initial blend (*split, spit*).

▶ *Special Note:* Point out that *threw* and *through* are pronounced the same but have different spellings and different meanings. Make sure students know what each word means.

B–C. Read the directions. Do the first one of each exercise with students. Let them complete the exercises independently or in pairs.

D. Read the directions. Using the completed example, review how to match a blend and a word family to make a real word. Remind students that the second word they write doesn't have to begin with a three-letter blend.

E. Review how to choose words to fill in the blanks. After students complete the exercise, have them read their sentences aloud.

▶ **Extending the skill:** Have students cut apart appropriate letter groups from PCM 14 and use them with letters and word families from PCM 13 to form new words.

Update Read or have students read this aloud. This is a good time to discuss health and fitness issues, including exercise, nutrition, and not smoking.

▶ **More Practice:** *Voyager 1 Workbook* p. 26

Help students fill out copies of PCM 15.

Lesson 9 (pp. 80–85)

Learning Goals Discuss the learning goals.

Before You Read Explain that students will use visualizing to better understand "Winner." Read the introduction. Discuss questions 1 and 2.

Key Words Ask students to read any baseball terms they recognize. Read the terms and definitions aloud and discuss them.

As You Read Read the strategy reminder aloud.

"Winner" Discuss the picture. Ask students if they can infer from the picture how the man feels about the boy's hit. Read the poem aloud. Then do a paired reading with students.

After You Read

A. Have students read the poem aloud, singly or in pairs.

B. Read and discuss the questions. *Optional:* Record students' retelling of the poem. Have them copy their version and read it aloud.

▶ **Extending the reading:** Have students work in small groups to discuss how students' parents reacted to their successes and/or how students react to their own children's successes. Ask, *"What pressures to succeed did you feel from your parents? What pressures do you place on your children?"*

Think About It: Making Inferences Remind students how we make inferences or "read between the lines." Discuss the examples. Ask, *"What clues lead to these inferences?"* Ask students if they can make any other inferences about the pictures. (e.g., "People are happy.") Record any new inferences and let students copy them.

Practice: Read the directions aloud. Demonstrate how to choose the better inference. Have students complete the exercise independently. Ask volunteers to explain why they chose each inference.

▶ **Extending the skill:** Using newspaper classified ads, have students look at "For Sale" advertisements and talk about what inferences they can make from the information (e.g., "size 3 designer wedding gown, never used," *inference:* a very thin rich woman didn't get married; "apartment sale, everything must go," *inference:* someone is moving and doesn't want these belongings).

Write About It: Write a Poem

A. Read the directions. Remind students that poets choose words carefully to convey strong visual and emotional messages. Have students share their thrilling experiences. If students can't think of a personal experience, suggest that they use something they know about. Brainstorm visual and other sensory words for the lines with the verbs *felt, see, hear,* and *taste.* Encourage students to be as descriptive as possible. Record responses on board and ask students to choose the words that best fit their own experience. Have them write those words on the lines in part **A.**

B. Help students decide what details they want to include in their poems. Then have them write their final poems in part **B.** Have them choose titles. Finally, have students read their poems aloud (see pages 11–12, "Working with Adult New Writers," for more ideas).

Word Work: Three-letter Final Blends (*nch, nce, nge, rse, dge*)

A–C. Follow the process described in Lesson 8. Point out that only two sounds are heard in most of these three-letter blends because *ch* is a digraph and the final *e* is silent. When students have completed part **C,** have them read the sentences aloud.

D. Review the definition of word families. Follow the process described in Lesson 1.

E. Read the directions. Have students work in pairs. Demonstrate how to read the sentence, find the clue, and unscramble the word in parentheses. Have students read the completed sentences aloud to emphasize that the unscrambled word rhymes with the clue word.

F. Read the directions. Scramble a word-family word on the board as an example. Then have partners scramble words for each other.

▶ **Extending the skill:** Have students cut apart appropriate letter groups from PCM 14 and use them with letters and word families from PCM 13 to form new words.

▶ **More Practice:** *Voyager 1 Workbook* p. 28

Help students fill out copies of PCM 15.

Writing Skills Mini-Lesson: Plurals (p. 86)

This mini-lesson focuses on rules for forming plurals. Read the introduction aloud. Explain plurals—words representing more than one person, place, or thing.

1. Read rule 1 and the examples. Write other examples on the board using words students have learned (*thrill/s, street/s, fence/s*).
2. Read rule 2 and examples; discuss it. Write other examples (*inch/es, dress/es, tax/es*).
3. Read and explain rule 3. Provide other examples (*strawberry/strawberries, party/parties, penny/pennies*).

Have students practice spelling plurals.

Practice: Have students complete the exercises as independently as possible. Have them explain why they spelled each plural as they did.

▶ **More Practice:** *Voyager 1 Workbook* p. 30

Unit 3 Review (pp. 87–88)

Follow the Unit Review process described in Unit 1. Point out that as students edit their writing they should check the spelling of plural words.

▶ **Extension:** Divide students into teams and conduct a word-forming contest. Have students use the letter groups they cut from PCM 13 and 14 to form words. See which team can form the most words in a given time period.

▶ **More Practice:** *Voyager 1 Workbook* p. 32

▶ *Final note:* Review with students the copies of PCM 15 that they have placed in their working folders. Ask what additional help they think they need with material from the three lessons and the writing skills mini-lesson in Unit 3. Discuss possible ways of meeting their needs.

▶ Unit 4: Friendship

Part of Unit	Voyager 1 pages	TRG pages	Workbook pages
Overview	89	58	
Lesson 10	90 – 95	58 – 59	34 – 35
Lesson 11	96 – 103	59 – 60	36 – 37
Lesson 12	104 – 111	60 – 61	38 – 39
Writing Skills Mini-Lesson	112	62	40 – 41
Unit 4 Review	113 – 114	62	42 – 44

Student Objectives

Reading
- Read four poems and a journal entry.
- Use the reading strategies of background knowledge, prior experience, and visualizing.
- Understand the main idea, find details, and make predictions.

Writing
- Write a poem and a journal entry; complete a diagram.
- Learn to add *-ed* and *-ing* endings to words.

Phonics
- Learn six special vowel combinations; *au, aw, oi, oy, oo, ou.*
- Learn nine *r*-controlled vowel patterns: *are, err, ire, ore, ure, ar, er, ear, our.*

▶ Unit 4 PCMs
PCM 10: Detail Diagram
PCM 13: Word Work (Units 1 and 2)
PCM 14: Word Work (Units 3 and 4)
PCM 15: Student Progress Tracking Sheet
PCM 18: Phonics Elements in *Foundation Book* and *Voyager 1*

▶ Personal Dictionaries and Spelling Lists
Encourage students to add words to their dictionaries and spelling lists during each lesson.

Unit 4 Overview (p. 89)

This overview introduces the theme of friendship. Discuss the picture and ask, *"What qualities do your friends have that make your friendships work?"* Read the overview aloud, then do a paired reading. For a second reading have students read aloud with you. Discuss the questions in the last paragraph.

Lesson 10 (pp. 90–95)

Learning Goals Discuss the learning goals.

Before You Read Explain that students will use what they know about arches and friendship to understand "The Arch." Read the introduction and discuss questions 1–3. Let students write their answers and read them aloud. Help students brainstorm and discuss common locations of arches. Discuss the attributes and uses of arches (very strong, an ancient building form, graceful, bear weight, their parts support each other).

Key Words See Lesson 1 notes. Explain that *-gh* is usually silent (*light, high, straight*) but that it sometimes has the *f* sound (*laugh, enough*). At the beginning of words, *gh* usually has the *g* sound.

As You Read Read the strategy reminder aloud.

"The Arch" Read the poem aloud. Then do a paired reading with students.

After You Read
A. Have students read the poem aloud, individually or in pairs.
B. Read each question and discuss it. For question 2, you may want to list pros and cons that students mention. For question 3, remind students that emotional responses may vary.

▶ Extending the reading
1. Have students brainstorm additional images that could represent friendship (a bouquet of

flowers, a knot, two people sitting in a small boat). Have students describe, verbally or in writing, how the images connote friendship.

2. Have students make a collage of images that, to them, symbolize friendship, using magazine pictures or their own drawings. Display their completed collages.

Think About It: Understanding the Main Idea

1. Read the introduction. Review the concept of main idea, the most important idea of a piece.

2. Reread "The Arch." Then read each stanza, followed by the phrase that summarizes the type of support mentioned.

3. Explain that the main idea is not always stated; it is often implied and must be inferred. Let students read "The Arch" again. Then let them restate the main idea in their own words.

Practice: Read the directions. After students read "Friends" silently, let them read it aloud. Then let them answer the question and explain their reasoning. Be sure to point out the difference between a main idea and supporting details.

▶ **Extending the skill:** Working in small groups, students can reread one of the selections in Unit 3 and write a sentence that states the main idea.

Write About It: Write a Poem

A. Read the introduction and "Smiles." Then let the class read it aloud. Discuss similarities and differences between "Smiles" and "The Arch."

B. Ask students to think of something that is like something else and complete the sentence. Encourage them to find a comparison that could be used in a poem about friendship.

C. On separate paper, have students expand on their comparisons. Then have them write their own poems. When they have drafted and titled their poems, have volunteers read them aloud. Let students revise the poems if they wish. They can then make a final draft on separate paper for their working folders (see pages 11–12).

Word Work: Special Vowel Combinations (au, aw, oi, oy, oo, ou) Use PCM 18 to review the long and short vowel sounds. Tell students that in this lesson they will learn about other vowel sounds.

A. Read the directions aloud. Read the heading of the first column aloud. Have students read aloud the words they know in this column. Read any other words in this column and have students repeat. Have students read the whole list. Ask volunteers to use each word in a sentence. Repeat this process for each list.

B. Read the directions. Have students read the words in the box. Remind them that the underlined word in each sentence has the same special vowel sound as the words that complete the sentence. Do the first one with students as an example and have them finish the exercise.

C. Read the directions. Repeat the strategy described in part **A**. Be sure students can distinguish between the different *oo* and *ou* sounds.

D. Read the directions; let students work independently or in pairs. Review how to choose words to fill in the blanks. Have students read their completed sentences aloud.

E. Follow the process described in Lesson 1.

F. Read the directions. Model an example of a simple rhyme if students need help.

▶ **Extending the skill:** Have students build new words using letters and word families from PCMs 13 and 14.

▶ **More Practice:** *Voyager 1 Workbook* p. 34

Help students fill out copies of PCM 15.

Lesson 11 (pp. 96–103)

Learning Goals Discuss the learning goals.

Before You Read Read the introduction. Explain that students will use their experiences to better understand three poems about friendship.

1. Tally the number of students who marked each choice. Let them read their additional choices.

2. Have students complete the sentence; discuss their responses.

Key Words See Lesson 1 notes. If students ask about the silent *t* in *listens*, explain that we don't pronounce the *t* when it appears in the middle of certain words (*fasten, glisten, soften, whistle*).

As You Read Read the strategy reminder aloud.

"A Special Friend" Read the poem aloud, then do a paired reading. Discuss the picture. Ask, *"In what ways does this illustrate the poem?"*

After You Read Explain that *friend's* is a contraction for *friend is*. Give other examples of contractions with the form "noun *is*" and use them in a sentence (The car's in the shop.) so that students don't confuse them with the possessive use of an apostrophe plus *s* (the car's engine).

A. Have each student read the poem aloud independently. Point out that, like the poet who wrote "Winner" in Lesson 9, this poet did not use conventional capitalization or punctuation.

B. Read the questions aloud and discuss them. Record student responses.

▶ **Extending the reading:** Have small groups of students talk about their special friendships.

Think About It: Finding Details Read the introduction aloud. Remind students that details support or explain the main idea. Have students reread "A Special Friend." Discuss how the main idea sentence is a summary of the ideas in the poem.

A. Read the directions. Have students check the details found in the poem and explain why they checked each one.

B. Read the introductory text. Explain the diagram: the topic is in the center oval; details describing it are in the outer boxes. Have students read the text in the diagram.

Practice

A–B. Read the directions. Let students read the poem aloud. Discuss unknown words. Have students reread the poem aloud on their own.

C. Have students answer the questions independently. Discuss their answers.

Write About It: Complete a Diagram

A. Read the introduction. Read the poem aloud, then conduct a paired or echo reading.

B. Read the questions aloud. Have students write their answers. Discuss the different details that students listed for question 3.

C. Discuss the diagram; have students read the text.

D. Before students begin, encourage them to think of qualities that make their friend special to them. Have students complete the diagram.

▶ **Extending the skill**

1. Let students draft a poem using their completed diagrams (see pages 11–12, "Working with Adult New Writers," for more ideas).

2. Have students complete PCM 10 with the main idea and details of "Friends" in Lesson 10 (page 92).

Word Work: *R*-controlled Vowels (*are, err, ire, ore, ure*) Use PCM 18 to review the long and short vowel sounds. Tell students they will learn how the letter *r* can change the way vowels sound.

A. Read the directions aloud. Say the sound for *-are* in column 1. Have students read the words they know in this column aloud. Read the other words and have students repeat them. Have students read the whole list aloud. Ask volunteers to use each word in a sentence. Repeat this process for each list.

B–C. Read the directions. Let students complete the exercises independently.

D. **Crossword Puzzle** Review the word list before students begin the puzzle. Show them how to fill in the blanks by using the clues. Students can work in pairs to do the puzzle.

▶ **Extending the skill:** Have students build new words using letters and word families from PCMs 13 and 14.

▶ **More Practice:** *Voyager 1 Workbook* p. 36

Help students fill out copies of PCM 15.

Lesson 12 (pp. 104–111)

Learning Goals Discuss the learning goals.

Before You Read Read the introduction aloud, or ask volunteers to read it. Explain that students will be using the strategy of visualizing to help them picture and understand what they read.

1. Read this question and discuss the picture. Have students write their predictions.

2. Explain that a journal is a book in which a person records personal thoughts, feelings, and ideas. Ask if students keep journals or know someone who does. Read and discuss the questions. Point out that by keeping a journal, students can improve their reading skills (by rereading entries) and practice their writing skills.
3. Have students list and discuss their reasons.

Key Words See Lesson 1 notes.

As You Read Read the strategy reminder aloud.

"Sofia's Journal" Follow one of the reading strategies on page 10.

After You Read
A. Start the retelling by saying *"Sofia had a busy week."* Go around the room and have volunteers add a sentence to the retelling of Sofia's story. Record each sentence as students dictate it. Continue until the story is complete. As a class, evaluate students' comprehension by comparing the retold version to the original.
B. Discuss the questions.

▶ **Extending the reading:** Ask students to think about something they have done recently that they would like to remember a year from now. In small groups, have them discuss things they might write in a journal. Ask, *"What can you record in a journal that can't be captured by photographs?"*

Think About It: Making Predictions Read and discuss the introduction. Have students copy and discuss their original prediction for Sofia's journal.

Practice
A. Read the directions. In pairs, have students read the titles and predictions and discuss which is the most reasonable prediction.
B–C. Read the directions. Have students complete these exercises with a partner and share their responses with the whole class.

▶ **Extending the skill:** Choose several easy-to-read newspaper articles, such as those in *News for You,* published by New Readers Press. Give students the article headlines to read. If photos accompany any of the articles, supply those as well.

In small groups, have students discuss the headlines and photos and predict what each article will be about. Then have them read the articles and compare their predictions with the actual content.

Write About It: Make a Journal Entry
A. Read and discuss the introduction. Have students read the journal entry silently. Then have students read the entry aloud.

Let students complete 1 and 2 individually. Then discuss them and compare answers as a group.

B. Read and discuss the introduction. Discuss different events that can bring about changes in a friendship, for better or for worse. Encourage students to list answers to the questions on separate paper. Have them brainstorm details and then draft a journal entry on the lines provided (see pages 11–12, "Working with Adult New Writers," for more ideas). If students prefer to write about an imaginary friendship, let them.

Word Work: More *R*-controlled Vowels (*ar, er, ear, our*) Remind students that the letter *r* can change the sounds of vowels it follows. Use PCM 18 to review the *r*-controlled vowel sounds students learned in Lesson 11 (*are, err, ire, ore, ure*).
A. Read the instructions. Say the three *-ar* words; have students repeat. Be sure they hear and say the different sounds. Have students read the sentences aloud. Read the exercise directions. Have a volunteer read the words in the box aloud. Let students work individually or in pairs to sort the words into the columns.
B–D. Repeat the process described in **A** for *er, ear,* and *our.* Read the directions for the exercises in these sections aloud; have students complete the exercises independently.

▶ **Extending the skill:** Have students build new words with their previously cut-apart letters and word families from PCMs 13 and 14.

▶ **More Practice:** *Voyager 1 Workbook* p. 38

Help students fill out copies of PCM 15.

Writing Skills Mini-Lesson: Adding *-ed* and *-ing* (p. 112)

This mini-lesson focuses on adding *-ed* and *-ing* endings to words. Explain that a word's use and tense can be changed by adding endings such as *-ed* and *-ing*. Provide examples. (*Warn* her/Tom is *warning* me/ I *warned* her yesterday.)

Read the introduction aloud.

1. Read rule 1 and the examples aloud. Write other examples on the board (*dreamed/dreaming, helped/helping*).
2. Read rule 2. Remind students that a silent *e* is an *e* at the end of a word that is not pronounced. Read the examples; write others on board (*liked/liking, saved/saving, shared/sharing*). Have volunteers provide other examples and write them on the board.
3. Read rule 3. If needed, remind students of the short vowel sounds. Read the examples. Write others on the board (*rub, sip, beg, spot, bat, pin*) and have students add *-ed* or *-ing*. Tell students that *w* and *x* are not doubled (*taxed, sewing*).

Practice: Read the directions. Have students complete these exercises independently. Ask them to explain why they used specific spellings. Have them name the specific rule they followed.

▶ **More Practice:** *Voyager 1 Workbook* p. 40

Unit 4 Review (pp. 113–114)

See Unit 1 Review notes. When students edit their writing, remind them to check that they added the *-ed* and *-ing* endings correctly.

▶ **More Practice:** *Voyager 1 Workbook* p. 42

▶ *Final note:* Review with students the copies of PCM 15 that they have placed in their working folders. Ask what additional help they think they need with material from the three lessons and the writing skills mini-lesson in Unit 4. Discuss possible ways of meeting their needs.

Skills Review (pp. 115–119)

When students have completed Unit 4, have them do the Skills Review. Encourage them to evaluate their own reading and writing progress by checking their answers against those given on page 119. They can use the Evaluation Chart on that page to identify any skill areas that need more work. Meet individually with students to go over their results. Have students complete the right side of the Student Interest Inventory on pages 6–7. Have them compare their answers to those they gave before beginning *Voyager 1* (see "Using the Skills Review" on page 42).

▶ **Alternative Final Assessment:** Follow the instructions on PCM 16: Tips for Preparing a Progress Portfolio to help students evaluate the material in their working folders and assemble progress portfolios for *Voyager 1*. Then use PCM 17: Portfolio Conference Questionnaire as you conduct one-on-one evaluation conferences with students.

Photocopy Masters

The following photocopy masters (PCMs) can be photocopied for classroom activities and homework. Here are brief suggestions for how to use them.

▶ PCMs for *Foundation Book*

▶ **PCM 1: Letter Formation Chart** Let students trace each letter, following the direction lines. Then have them practice forming the letters.

▶ **PCM 2: Student Progress Tracking Sheet** Use this PCM each time students finish a lesson. Have students write words they've learned. Have them dictate answers to the other sections and keep the sheets in their working folders.

▶ **PCMs 3–7: Units 1–5 Words** Have students cut apart the PCM 3 words. Demonstrate how to build a sentence with the words. (*The cab is full.*)

You may want to group the words by part of speech to make sentence building easier. Point out that each sentence should start with a capitalized word. Continue to add to the word bank with PCMs 4, 5, 6, and 7.

▶ **PCM 8: Letters, Consonant Blends, and Word Families** Have students cut the letters and word families apart. Demonstrate how to use them to form words, starting with consonants and short-vowel word families (*s* + *un* = *sun*). Help students to create and read each new word aloud. Add the blends and longer word families as appropriate.

▶ PCMs for *Voyager 1*

▶ **PCM 9: Five W's Chart** Use with Lessons 5 and 8 to help students find or gather details.

▶ **PCM 10: Detail Diagram** Use with Lessons 5, 8, and 11 to help students identify details in what they read or to brainstorm details while prewriting.

▶ **PCM 11: Cause-and-Effect Chart** Use with Lessons 2 and 7 to help students identify cause and effect in what they read, or to help them organize a cause-and-effect narrative while prewriting.

▶ **PCM 12: Sequence Time Line** Use with Lessons 1 and 8 to help students identify the sequence of events in what they read or to help them organize a sequential narrative while prewriting.

▶ **PCMs 13–14: Word Work** Have students cut the letters and letter groups apart. Demonstrate how to form words, starting with a consonant and a short word family (*f* + *an* = *fan*). Help students create and read each new word aloud. Add blends and longer word families as appropriate.

▶ **PCM 15: Student Progress Tracking Sheet** Have students complete this PCM each time they finish a lesson. You may need to write their dictated answers. Students should save these tracking sheets in their working folders.

▶ **PCM 16: Tips for Preparing a Progress Portfolio** Use this PCM to help students prepare their portfolios. Discuss each question and option with students. The process of preparing a portfolio may take quite a while. Show students PCM 17 before you schedule a conference.

▶ **PCM 17: Portfolio Conference Questionnaire** Schedule individual conferences. At each conference, discuss the questions on PCM 17. Write notes on the PCM. Put a copy of the completed PCM in the student's portfolio.

▶ **PCM 18: Phonics Elements in *Foundation Book* and *Voyager 1*** Use this as a reference tool. Students may highlight each phonics element as they learn it.

Letter Formation Chart

A A a a a   B B b b   C C c c

D D d d   E E e e   F F f f

G G g g   H H h h   I I i i

J J j j   K K k k   L L l l

M M m m   N N n n   O O o o

P P p p   Q Q q q   R R r r

S S s s   T T t t   U U u u

V V v v   W W w w   X X x x

Y Y y y   Z Z z z

Student Progress Tracking Sheet

Name: _____

Lesson: _____

Date started: _____ Date ended: _____

New words I learned: _____

_____

_____

_____

_____

What I liked best about the lesson: _____

_____

_____

_____

What I need more practice with: _____

_____

_____

_____

Unit 1 Words

Cut these words apart. Make sentences with the words.

A	desk	friends	He	open
a	dig	full	his	put
An	Don	garage	hold	puts
an	door	garden	hose	shade
and	drink	gate	house	subway
August	drinks	give	in	Sunday
bank	eat	gives	is	The
book	eats	grow	jacket	the
bookstore	fast	grows	Jan	them
bus	fish	Gus	July	They
cab	food	Hal	May	to
can	Frank	half	new	up
closed	french fries	hand	office	vegetables
coffee	Friday	has	old	wagon
December	friend	have	on	window

▶ PCM 3

Foundation Book

Unit 2 Words

Cut these words apart. Make sentences with the words. Use words
from Unit 1, too.

answer	easy	likes	pays	Stan
are	for	love	pipe	stop
at	get	man	plumber	their
be	gets	March	problem	truck
calls	go	Maria	quart	Tuesday
car	happy	Monday	question	Vicky
children	her	money	quiet	want
clean	into	morning	quiz	wants
clothes	It	movie	rainy	water
come	it	must	Ramon	Wednesday
day	key	Nancy	She	will
dinner	kids	neighbor	show	with
drip	labor	next	so	woman
drive	Laundromat	park	some	work
drives	laundry	pay	square	works

Unit 3 Words

Cut these words apart. Make sentences with the words. Use words from Units 1 and 2, too.

All	hard	Sandy	takes	very
all	help	school	telephone	walk
am	helps	September	television	walks
birthday	I	sidewalk	tell	wash
box	job	sister	tells	Wayne
cake	June	sisters	Then	wet
city	large	soda	then	woods
dear	November	start	This	yawns
exercise	October	starts	this	year
exit	of	stove	Tony	yell
February	order	study	too	yells
feel	orders	suitcase	train	yield
feels	party	swim	trip	You
GED	pencil	swims	valentine	you
good	pizza	take	vase	zipper

Foundation Book

Unit 4 Words

Cut these words apart. Make sentences with the words. Use words from Units 1, 2, and 3, too.

apple	Do	January	Pat	shed
as	does	jobs	pet	sit
back	dog	jug	picks	soon
bed	down	just	plug	sound
bill	fed	kick	push	spell
bit	fill	learning	quick	stuck
block	flat	less	quit	sub
but	fog	lunch	quite	sun
cat	grill	makes	red	thick
chips	ham	mess	rock	top
club	hat	mop	rub	until
cold	hill	my	run	well
cook	hit	nap	sat	when
cop	hug	not	Saturday	write
dip	jam	now	sell	yet

Unit 5 Words

Cut these words apart. Make sentences with the words. Use words
from Units 1, 2, 3, and 4, too.

again	crumb	grand	see	spaghetti
applies	diploma	hold	sees	spill
April	drag	keep	shop	steam
better	drop	off	skates	stick
bless	family	over	ski	stir
blot	Find	past	skid	sweep
break	finds	plan	slap	Thursday
Bring	flip	plans	sleep	Today
brings	floor	pot	sleeps	today
broom	flowers	press	slope	tree
brush	fresh	program	smell	tries
closet	glad	programs	smog	try
clutter	glass	proud	smoke	turn
crock	gloom	rules	snap	twenty
crop	graduation	sauce	snow	twice

▶ **PCM 7**

Letters, Consonant Blends, and Word Families

Cut these letters and word families apart. Make words.

a	b	c	d	e	f
g	h	i	j	k	l
m	n	o	p	q	r
s	t	u	v	w	x
y	z	bl	br	cl	cr
dr	fl	fr	gl	gr	pl
pr	sl	sm	sp	st	sk
sn	tr	tw	am	at	ap
ab	ag	ass	and	ack	an
ed	ell	ess	et	esh	ick
ill	ip	it	im	in	ob
ock	og	op	oom	ub	uff
ug	un	um	uck	ump	ush

Five W's Chart

Who?	_____ _____
What?	_____ _____
Where?	_____ _____
When?	_____ _____
Why?	_____ _____

▶ PCM 9

Detail Diagram

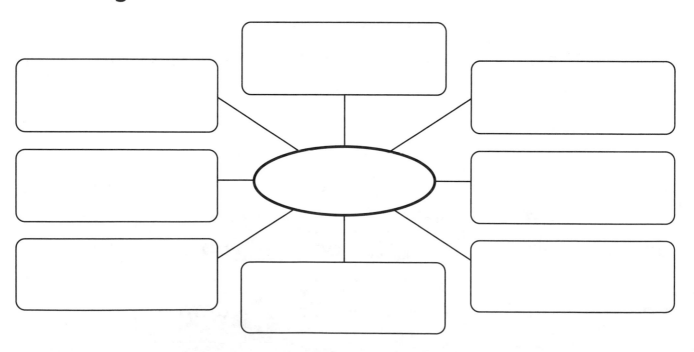

▶ PCM 10

Cause-and-Effect Chart

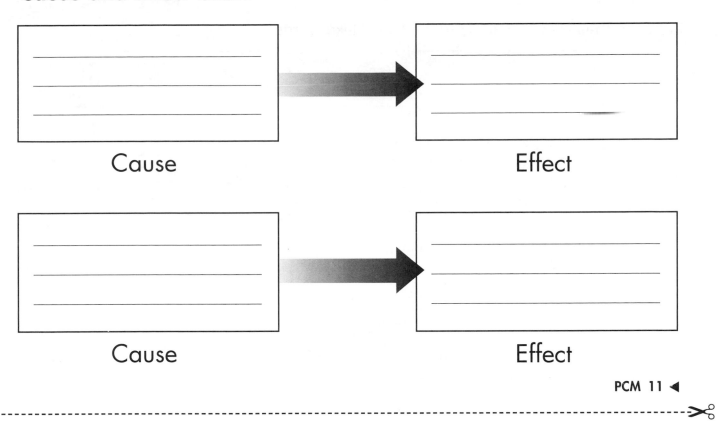

Cause → Effect

Cause → Effect

- ✂

Sequence Time Line

1.   **2.**   **3.**   **4.** →

First
you are born.

Second
you are a child.

Then
you are a teen.

Last
you are an adult.

1.   **2.**   **3.**   **4.** →

First   Second   Then   Last

_____ _____ _____ _____

_____ _____ _____ _____

_____ _____ _____ _____

Word Work (Units 1 and 2)

Cut apart these letters and word families. Make words.

a	b	c	d	e
f	g	h	i	j
k	l	m	n	o
p	q	r	s	t
u	v	w	y	z
br	cl	gr	pl	st
ad	en	id	ot	un
an	ass	ing	op	ub
ft	ld	mp	nt	st
amp	est	old	ift	ump
ail	ain	ake	ace	ame
ice	ine	ite	ight	ind
each	ead	eat	eed	eak
oat	old	one	ore	use

Word Work (Units 3 and 4)

Cut these digraphs, word families, and letter groups apart. Make words. Use letters and letter groups from PCM 13, too.

ch	sh	th	ph	wh
scr	spl	spr	str	thr
one	eat	in	en	ine
ain	int	ead	eam	ew
nch	nce	nge	rse	dge
ance	ench	inch	inge	edge
au	aw	oi	oy	oil
ook	ool	ound	are	err
ire	ore	ure	ar	er
ear	our	all	ask	ack
eet	ent	ess	ide	ill
ope	oss	ush	ust	unch

Student Progress Tracking Sheet

Name: _____

Lesson: _____

Date started: _____ Date ended: _____

What I learned from the reading: _____

_____

_____

_____

What I learned from **Think About It**: _____

_____

_____

_____

What I learned from **Write About It**: _____

_____

_____

_____

What I liked about the lesson: _____

_____

What I need more practice with: _____

_____

_____

Voyager 1

Tips for Preparing a Progress Portfolio

Your Progress Portfolio will show what you have learned in *Voyager 1*. Follow these tips as you prepare your portfolio.

1. Photocopy your completed Student Interest Inventory. Put it in your Progress Portfolio folder.

2. Look at all the material in your working folder. Pick out the items you would like to put in your Progress Portfolio. Be sure to include all of the Student Progress Tracking Sheets that you completed for *Voyager 1*.

3. Here is a list of the writings you have done in *Voyager 1*.

Lesson 1: a list	**Lesson 7:** a story
Lesson 2: a poem	**Lesson 8:** a list
Lesson 3: a poem	**Lesson 9:** a poem
Unit 1 Review: your dream	**Unit 3 Review:** a thrilling moment
Lesson 4: write about a reading	**Lesson 10:** a poem
Lesson 5: interview and write	**Lesson 11:** a detail diagram
Lesson 6: a paragraph	**Lesson 12:** a journal entry
Unit 2 Review: a hero	**Unit 4 Review:** a special friend

Pick the pieces you would like to put in your portfolio. Make sure your name, a title, and the date it was written are on each piece of writing. List the pieces of writing you picked on a separate paper. Put the list with the pieces of writing in your folder.

4. Think about the skills you have learned. List the skills pages you would like to put in your portfolio:

Think About It pages:_____

Word Work pages:_____

Writing Skills Mini-Lesson pages: _____

Photocopy these pages. Make sure your name and a date are on each page. Make a separate list of these pages. Put the list with the pages in your folder.

5. If you would like, photocopy your Personal Dictionary and put it in your portfolio.

6. Look through the items in your Progress Portfolio. Read the questions on PCM 17. Think about answers to these questions as you prepare for your portfolio conference.

Portfolio Conference Questionnaire

To the instructor: Use this questionnaire as you conduct portfolio conferences with students.

Student: _____ Date: _____

Instructor: _____ Course: _____

1. Which items did you choose for your portfolio?

2. Why did you choose these items?

3. What do they show that you have learned?

4. What things are you most proud of?

5. What would you like to do better?

6. What would you like to do more of?

7. What do you still need to do to reach your educational goals?

Phonics Elements in *Foundation Book* and *Voyager 1*

Consonants

Consonant Letters that Represent One Sound

b	book	**l**	laundry	**s**	sister
d	door	**m**	man	**t**	train
f	food	**n**	Nancy	**v**	valentine
h	hill	**p**	pipe	**w**	water
j	jacket	**qu**	quiz	**x**	box
k	key	**r**	rain	**y**	yell
				z	zip

Consonant Letters that Represent More than One Sound

g	garden, giant	**c**	car, city

Common Consonant Blends

Common 2–Letter Initial Blends

bl	blot	**gl**	glad	**st**	stove
br	bring	**gr**	grand	**sk**	ski
cl	closet	**pl**	plan	**sn**	snow
cr	crop	**pr**	press	**tr**	trip
dr	drop	**sl**	slap	**tw**	twin
fl	flip	**sm**	smell		
fr	Frank	**sp**	spill		

Common 3–Letter Initial Blends

scr	scrap
spl	split
spr	sprain
str	strain
thr	three

Common 2–Letter Final Blends

ft	gift
ld	old
mp	lamp
nt	cent
st	best

Common 3–Letter Final Blends

nch	inch
nce	once
nge	change
rse	nurse
dge	edge

Consonant Digraphs

ch	chin	**th**	than
sh	ship	**ph**	phone
		wh	why

Phonics Elements in *Foundation Book* and *Voyager 1*

Vowels

Vowel Letters and the Sounds They Represent

Vowel	Short Sound	Long Sound
a	cat	gave
e	pet	me
i	fish	ride
o	job	hope
u	bug	use, June
y		any, my

Common Vowel Combinations and the Sounds They Represent

Long Vowel Sounds		Other Vowel Sounds	
ai	paid	au	auto
ay	day	aw	saw
ee	need	ea	head
ea	each, great	oi	oil
igh	high	oy	boy
oe	toe	oo	book
oa	goat	ou	about
oo	too		
ou	you		
ue	argue, due		

Common *R*–controlled Vowels and the Sounds They Represent

are	dare	ar	arm, warm, marry
err	berry	er	very, hero, her
ire	hire	ear	hear, wear, heard
ore	more	our	our, four, journey
ure	cure		